"This is a bold and imaginative work, brilliantly researched, penetrating to the core of the question that confronts us all: Who are we? What are we?

"Knowing who we are and what we are is both the question and in some ways the ultimate answer. We are about the exploration of ourselves—we are that discovering. It is the brilliance of Donovan and Joiner-Bey that turn this quest into a finely woven tapestry of ideas and visions.

"Framed amid this New Age adventure, free will finds its purpose and we find our meaning. It is the enabler, basic to the author's vision. 'Life evolves and unfolds to become self-aware and realize its full potential.'

"This is a New Age masterpiece—clear, thorough. In their study they weave the fabric of both religion and science, creating a new view of our reality. We are both place and role in the patterns that Donovan and Joiner-Bey reveal. And in the end we are not left to wonder what the answer is to the questions with which they begin their journey. Their search is a journey that carries you to the end and in the end you find the answer. Who am I? Donovan and Joiner-Bey answer."

Evan Harris Walker, Ph. D.,
Physicist and author of The Physics of Consciousness
and founder of the Walker Cancer Institute

"Most impressive! It has almost everything in it. The material is so rich... Such a probing and deep work it might 'freak out' some academic and professional colleagues as well as move some very profoundly as you back metaphysics with detailed observation."

Z'ev ben Shimon Halevi, Director of the Kabbalah Society ,
Author of The Way of Kabbalah, A Kabbalistic Universe,
and numerous other books on Kabbalah and cosmology

"In answering the questions, 'Who am I? What am I? and Why am I here?' Doctors Patrick Donovan and Herb Joiner-Bey weave us through a course on mysticism, mythology, archetypes, religion, history, quantum physics, physical chemistry, chaos theory, fractal geometry, and psychoneuroimmunology. They tackle dualities of the universe: I/Thou, part/whole, self/others, humanity/divinity, wave/particle, yin/yang, man/woman, good/evil, health/illness, and weave through their lessons teachings from the *Kabbalah,* the *Bible,* the Egyptian *Book of the Dead,* the Hindu *Rig Veda,* the *Tao Te Ching,* the *I Ching,* Carl Jung, systems theory, and ancient Celtic stone carvings.

"Their research is exhaustive and scholarly, and yet their writing is friendly—they hold your hand and lead you through these complex and diverse terrains. What they end up delivering is a remarkable integration and synthesis, a whole-world view of consciousness and being. They distill out the simple truths and destinations we are all seeking: self-identity, self-affirmation, personal destiny, and connection to a greater whole."

Ralph T. Golan, M.D., Author of
Optimal Wellness: Where Mainstream and Alternative Meet

"I wish *The Face of Consciousness* had been available when I was a young clinician—I could have learned the art of healing much sooner and better helped so many more patients. This work is transformational, not just for practitioners, but to each of us on our unique, personal journey through life. Ultimately, isn't full manifestation of our "selfness" or "consciousness" all we really have? Exploring this wonderful book has been a powerful experience. It will be a powerful experience for you as well.

"I can think of no better reward for a teacher than to be taught by his students. Thank you Dr. Patrick Donovan, thank you Dr. Herb Joiner-Bey for making all the hard work worthwhile."

Joseph E. Pizzorno, Jr. N.D.,
President Emeritus, Bastyr University,
Editor, Integrative Medicine: A Clinician's Journal,
Author of Total Wellness *and*
Co-author of The Textbook of Natural Medicine

"Your book appears to have both inner and outer structures. It strikes me that the outward structure of your book consists of the explicit references to ideas and their relationships that come from science, philosophy and spirituality. But the inner structure is more consistent with that of poetry. Possibly the term 'prosetry' would be more apt. Prosetry: pros that has the effect of poetry on the reader's mind. Poetry (and prosetry) can elevate our perspectives. This form of literature wherever found, helps us to appreciate the subtle, but still profound, aspects of our realities.

"I hope your book will be adopted by curriculums in the naturopathic community since it seems to provide a model I am referring to. Your book invites readers to engage it with their own thoughts and feelings while trying to abstract meaning from its pages. During that exchange, readers have the opportunity to further evolve and refine their own conceptual frameworks for subsequent practice and action. To the extent that it would be used to assist students in becoming more mindful of their emotional lives as they relate to the topics in the book, so much the better."

Ken Ostrander, Ed.D.
Professor of Education (retired), University of Washington

"I feel you have done a very profound, solid and rigorous inquiry into the nature of consciousness and this is the kind of book that I would be happy to recommend. In significant ways I can also see that it is complimentary to my own work as it goes in depth where I have not. Your study of how disease may be related to consciousness on a larger scale is very interesting."

Carl Johan Calleman, Ph.D., Internationally recognized expert on the Mayan calendar and author of The Mayan Calendar, *and* The Mayan Calendar and the Transformation of Consciousness

The Face of Consciousness
A Guide to Self-Identity and Healing

PATRICK DONOVAN, N.D.
HERBERT JOINER-BEY, N.D.

Lucky Press

LUCKY PRESS, LLC ~ LANCASTER, OHIO

[Handwritten inscription:]

To Terry & Maurene:

It is good to again recognise and enjoy the company of old souls & old friends. Blessings and many a good salmon dinner shared again!

Patrick

FIRST EDITION
Printed on acid-free paper

Publisher's website: www.luckypress.com
Dr. Donovan's website: www.pdonovan.com

ISBN-10: 0-9776300-1-3
ISBN-13: 978-0-9776300-1-1

PLEASE SEE CREDITS ON PAGE 242.

Book design by Janice Marie Phelps

Library of Congress Cataloging-in-Publication Data
Donovan, Patrick, 1951–
    The face of consciousness : a guide to self-identity and healing / Patrick Donovan. -- 1st ed.
        p. cm.
    Includes bibliographical references and index.
    ISBN-13: 978-0-9776300-1-1 (trade pbk. : alk. paper)
    ISBN-10: 0-9776300-1-3 (trade pbk. : alk. paper)
    1. Consciousness. 2. Self. 3. Identity (Philosophical concept)
    4. Healing. 5. Spirituality. I. Joiner-Bey, Herb. II. Title.
    B105.C477D66 2006
    126--dc22
                                    2006010216

In memory of my beloved friend and teacher Ruth Johnson.

*For my parents (Esther and Bill), Janet,
my children Erin & Connor, and
all who ask the question and
live "The Journey."*

Table of Contents

Foreword

Joseph E. Pizzorno, Jr. N.D.
President Emeritus, Bastyr University
Editor, *Integrative Medicine: A Clinician's Journal*

"The patient does not come to the doctor to be cured; the patient comes to be known"—A profound insight. This concept never occurred to me in the early days of my practice. While well trained in the art and science of natural healing by the great healer/teachers John Bastyr, DC, ND, Joe Boucher, ND, Bob Carroll, ND and so many others, it took me years of clinical practice before I became aware that many of my patients came to see me for more than physical healing.

Sadly, we live in a world suffering from a tremendous burden of unnecessary sickness and pain. Much of that is clearly in the physical world: the incidence of most chronic degenerative diseases has increase in almost every age group every decade the past fifty years. Much of that is due to our increasingly polluted environment and the decreasing nutrient value of the foods we eat (still plenty of calories, but fewer nutrients). Equally important has been the startling failure of conventional medicine to improve health in stark contrast to its almost miraculous ability to safe lives. This failure of medicine is due largely to its orientation to the diagnosis and treatment of disease rather than improvement of the health of the patient. Therein lies naturopathic medicine's greatest strength—our fundamental belief in the health potential of each person who comes to us for care.

This inherent striving of living organisms towards health has been named in many ways: I like the *vis medicatrix naturae,* or "healing power of nature." It is a powerful force within each of us. But this force is not simply a manifestation of biochemistry, it is a manifestation of life in all its aspects.

I remember vividly, now twenty-five years later, my sudden insight into a woman who had been seeing me for almost a year. I do not recall her first diagnosis, nor her second or third. Each time she came to see me with a well-characterized, easily diagnosable disease. Each time, using nutrition and botanical medicines, I helped her eliminate her disease and apparently return to health. However, when she came to see me for her fourth, different disease in less than a year, I suddenly realized I was treating the wrong problem. I started to listen to her more carefully, not just to her symptoms. What I heard was a person no one listened to, saw a person unrecognized, and felt a person unloved and unloving. I suddenly understood that she was coming to me, an authority figure, to be heard, seen, appreciated—told she was important, of value—real.

It was a stunning revelation to me. I had prided myself in being a good doctor, competent in my diagnosis of pathology and expert in determining the underlying physiological dysfunction that lead to a patient's ill health and susceptibility to disease. I was also very good at utilizing the many effective therapies of natural medicine to facilitate normal function and restore health. But I was not yet a healer. I did not yet understand how to elicit within my patient the full manifestation of her lifeforce, spirit—selfness. I totally changed the way I interacted with this woman. I still provided the expected, and necessary, diagnostic and therapeutic care she needed. However, I also started spending more time listening to her, guided her to find a pathway to exploration of her spiritual self. No, I did not recommend to her any specific religion or spiritual guide, but rather helped her recognize the necessity of manifesting this aspect of her life and she then found her own way. As she found the meaning and importance of her life, she soon came to no longer need my services. She was healed, not just cured. And I took another step in my journey becoming a healer/physician, an unending, but deeply rewarding experience.

I wish *The Face of Consciousness* had been available when I was a young clinician—I could have learned the art of healing much sooner and better helped so many more patients. This work is transformational, not just for practitioners, but to each of us on our unique, personal journey through life. Ultimately, isn't full manifestation of our "selfness" or "consciousness" all we really have? Exploring this wonderful book has been a powerful experience. It will be a powerful experience for you as well.

I can think of no better reward for a teacher than to be taught by his students. Thank you Dr. Patrick Donovan, thank you Dr. Herb Joiner-Bey for making all the hard work worthwhile.

Preface

Who are you and why are you here? Why is anyone or anything "here," living in this world, this universe? Better yet, why is there anything at all, even a "here?" Life forms come and go, eventually to be lost to the dark abyss of the evolutionary obsolete. Even you and your loved ones come and go, each a mere microsecond on the time line of eternity. It all seems so useless, so meaningless! But why is it so?

Many authors have written about the evolution of life, "consciousness," the cosmology of the universe, the "new physics," the biology of living systems, the mythology of life's "Sacred Quest" and the hero's journey, and the mystical experience of life's transformation through death into new life. Their information has been innovative and often inspirational. However, few have attempted to engage the "why" behind the scientifically quantified phenomena of life and the physical universe. Because of this, the issues of causation and reason relative to the development of life, consciousness, identity and self-awareness have not been explicitly addressed to any great degree.

One can discern specific reasons for this situation and the obstacles to integrating experience and insight across scientific and theological disciplines. Since the time of Descartes and the Scientific Revolution, which finalized the separation of faith and reason, Western scientists have been loath, in fear of professional suicide, to explore realms culturally sequestered to the exclusive purview of theologians. Conversely, unbridled scientific inquiry has been a terrifying anathema among clerics and the "religious faithful" for fear any philosophical or rational inquiry or dialogue would open the door to "the devil of doubt and reason." Consequently, no well-defined, unifying theory of causation or reason for existence has been postulated addressing all of the various disciplines from science to mythology and mysticism using a language that integrates their essential precepts into a functional hypothesis offering significant personal, social, and therapeutic applicability.

With the help of Dr. Joiner-Bey, I wrote this book in an attempt to transcend and neutralize the culturally conditioned barriers and perception of antagonism among the many schools of thought regarding the "why" of creation, consciousness, healing and the Cosmos. We labored to dissolve these arbitrary barriers and the resulting fragmented, territorial thinking by coherently integrating the strikingly similar, irreducible pearls of truth, residing consistently at the core of these paradigms, into a unifying theory of creation, life and the transformational process of healing.

This unifying theory is predicated upon the primary theme of self-realized identity arising from these historically antagonistic, yet remarkably parallel paths of revelation. The verified quantifiable properties of living systems, as described by modern physicists and biologists, are conceptually matched by the ancient discoveries and understandings of philosophers and mystics. The fabric of this "unified theory of life" is woven from these parallel threads and based on; 1) the mystical traditions and scientific evidence pinpointing consciousness as the fundamental phenomenon (the "Materia Prima") of life and, 2) the conclusion that the primal driving force of life (its "raison d'etre") is its "sacred quest," as consciousness, for a sense of its own identity i.e., a realization of itself through the experience of itself. I feel Dr. Joiner-Bey and I have formulated a new perspective on consciousness and its manifestation as life through the synthesis of essential principles from the biological and physical sciences, psychology, philosophy, mythology and various traditional schools of mystical thought (e.g., Kabbalah, Sufism, etc.). In addition, we propose a theory that explains the "why" of creation and life and defines the transformational process of healing in a way in which it can be practically applied to one's life enabling one to transcend death and transform illness into greater life.

This book is only a beginning. There is so much more yet to be researched, experienced and written. This book is our initial endeavor to promote individual exploration and personal revelation, and to nurture integrative thinking and dialogue among scholars, healers, and the general public. We wish to encourage more vigorous, unlimited, and fruitful dialogue among scientists, philosophers, theologians and every individual seeking answers to his/her own existence. Perhaps then, the fragmented half-truths and dogmatic exclusivisms that have dominated discussions of the most haunting questions of the human heart and mind can be transcended by a clearer and more satisfying picture of who we are and why we are here.

Patrick M. Donovan, N.D.

Introduction:

They Come To Be Known

"The patient does not come to the doctor to be cured; the patient comes to be known." This profound statement slipped innocently from the lips of my friend and colleague Leanna Standish, Ph.D., N.D., L.Ac, as she addressed the graduating class of naturopathic physicians at Bastyr University. There I was, sitting quietly on stage with the other faculty members, my eyes wandering through the sea of nameless faces in the audience, wondering if the atmosphere at yet another graduation was going to get any stuffier. Then I heard it: "The patient comes to be known." Like a sudden gust of cool wind that throws open the doors on a quiet August evening announcing the onset of a sudden summer storm, this statement of revelation threw open the doors of my mind with its gust of confirmation.

That was it! What I had been considering for some time, through years of study in various mystical traditions, as the primal cause for the creation of the universe may also be the key factor through which healing could be defined and illness and disease could be understood. Identity is the unifying key. Self-realization and the quest for meaning are the stimulus for creation, the evolution of self-aware consciousness and the unfolding of life through the cosmogonic cycle of continuous creation and transformational change. Therefore, realizing and living passionately one's true, essential nature of being is the key to healing. The essential question that resounds throughout the soul of every sentient, self-aware being throughout the universe is a question of identity—"Who or What Am I?"

The more I thought about it the more familiar the question became. Actually, I realized most of us know it very well. Sometimes friend, sometimes foe, it regularly, consciously cries out in the midst of adolescent emotional traumas and haunts the intimacy of every meaningful relationship we have. More often we ignore it or actively suppress it within the shadows of our subconscious. Answering it is a frightening proposition. Most of us choose to battle with the feelings of anxiety, fear, loneliness, and isolation that arise from its suppression—feelings commonly associated with illness and overwhelmingly present in the lives of the majority of my patients.

Now, sitting in that graduation ceremony, those nameless faces in the crowd seemed so much more familiar as I realized, in that moment, we all come into the experience of life to be known to ourselves and to others. Through that act of knowing, we are made whole—we are healed.

The Question

The most fundamental question of life and of the consciousness that animates life is the question of identity. It is the quintessential question of every self-aware being and the fundamental query that lies at the very root of consciousness. The urge to answer this query is the impetus that, through the illusory experience of separation, continuously drives the individualized, self-aware consciousness of the I to enter into relationship with itself and the universe as Thou. This impulse forces the ego to ultimately "lose itself" in the illusion of separateness that it may "find itself" in the reality of wholeness. For anyone to answer the question of identity fully is to realize the "why" of creation and to know who one is as a conscious participant in that creation.

Many mystical traditions propose that the question of identity is the very causal phenomenon that motivates the unrealized potential of God, The Absolute All, into the act of creating. Through this act, "The Face" is able to "gaze upon The Face," and "God beholds God" and rejoices in His glory and magnificence. The dynamic, ever-evolving process of life is generated and propagated by the asking and answering of this question. Its query is the root of the "Sacred Quest" of the mythic hero—the mythological representation and male archetype of ego-consciousness seeking to discover its true essential nature of being. Additionally, self-realization is intimately related to the transformational process that brings about healing.

As I further pondered the question of identity—its biological, psychological, mythological, and theological implications—I turned to my close friend and colleague, Dr. Herb Joiner-Bey for more inspiration and intelligent dialogue. Many lengthy conversations ensued which led to a remarkable discourse ultimately resulting in this book.

The Process

To answer the question of identity, we explored the latest scientific evidence and theories pertaining to the origins and nature of living systems, particularly in the disciplines of physics, biology, and mathematics. We reviewed the mythological, theological and mystical concepts of cosmogony and the nature of life in the light of the scientific information, hoping to develop a richer, more complete understanding of the origin and nature of consciousness, of the self, as it manifests individually and universally as life. Our explorations have only begun to scratch the surface of the information available. We confess that so much more has yet to be done. But, because we have been so impressed by the recurring themes and patterns of conception, belief, and evidence, over such wide-ranging disciplines and perspectives, uncovered at every level of investigation, we felt compelled to share what we have gathered so far.

The Thesis

We believe the purpose of life is to give identity and meaning to consciousness. We believe the recurring patterns observed in physics, metaphysics, and biology constitute a unique and unmistakable "signature," "fingerprint," or "hallmark" of identity, revealing the true essential nature of the Infinite Self that brought life into being. We also believe the fundamental principles or archetypes of life that determine and govern the nature and function of living systems are the functional constructs of this fingerprint and should act as the foundation upon which a more complete and functional understanding of health and healing is based. We propose that the fundamental patterns of living systems are the fingerprints of life—evidence of the "Creator's" personality and identity. By understanding them in this context, one can recognize the "Deity" within each creation and begin to answer the primordial, burning question of self-awareness—"Who or What Am I?"

The Book

In the following pages, we present the results of our exploration in a synopsis to acquaint you with what we feel to be the salient principles of life and the true fundamental nature of being and of healing. It is our fervent hope that our presentation will stimulate further exploration, discussion, and illumination by you and others. Hopefully, this exposition will give you a sense of connectedness to something greater than the separate *I* of the ego-self and provide a more comprehensive understanding and knowledge of the laws of causality, transformation and healing. We would be delighted if this awareness serves as a springboard to propel you towards an expanded appreciation of your own unique identity as a distinctive part of the Divine Whole. May this new self-realization assist you in answering the question "Who or What am I?" and catalyze a healing and self-affirming transformation.

SECTION I:
Wholeness and the Grand Illusion

Chapter 1

A Question of the Soul

"To be, or not to be—that is the question:
Whether 'tis nobler in the mind, to suffer
The slings and arrows of outrageous fortune,
Or take arms against a sea of troubles,
And by opposing end them?"

William Shakespeare,
Hamlet; Act III. Scene I.

The "Sacred Quest"

There has been a story being told since the beginning of time. It is the story of you and me. It is our story. It is the story of all of life and the consciousness life embodies. Its plot is simple: "Reflect Me that I may see My 'Self' and know I AM." The characters are infinite and diverse; they include the life-forms of all living systems from the simplest and most minute to the grandest and most complex. They are constantly changing and evolving, always struggling to survive against the unremitting influences of death and non-being and their own self-generated illusions of separateness and isolation merely to realize in the end only birth conquers death and only love shatters the illusion of separateness. There is, however, an irony here. For only through death can the mystery behind the plot of life's story be revealed, and only through the illusion of separateness can self be reflected in the face of another to realize that beneath the illusion of twins dwells the reality of oneness.

But who or what is this thing called "self?" Herein lies the mystery of our story. It is deeply rooted in this question and the more fundamental question of identity: "Who or what am I?" This question of identity is a question of self-aware consciousness that also intimates a question of origin ("Whence came I?") and a question of purpose ("Why am I here?"). It is bound closely with beginnings and commonly appears as the catalyst stirring the eternal stillness into manifest existence in numerous creation stories and myths. Every character in the story of life arriving upon the threshold of self-consciousness is faced with this mystery and must answer this inevitable question of the soul. Answering it truthfully demands wholehearted and profound introspection and a passionate love and almost obsessive curiosity for life. It also demands the willingness and fortitude to manifest and experience the answer fully in one's life; discovering its answer is not a singular, momentary revelational event: it is the activity of life itself. One lives the continual query as a state of consciousness, as a state of being and becoming where one is ever watchful for and receptive to the answer. The asking and answering of this question is the dynamic, ever-evolving phenomenon that writes life's story—our story. The search for the answer to the question of identity is the sacred quest of life and the consciousness that is life. Life itself is the answer.

"The Quest" of all mystical and mythological journeys from all cultures and peoples may very well be representative of life's sacred quest for identity through self-realization. This quest is often exemplified in the myths of the hero where the common theme is one of life's resurrection into greater life through the death that transforms life. For this to occur, the pre-hero, as commoner, must undertake a perilous journey replete with some great deed(s) of self-sacrifice through which his/her life is transfigured into "The Divine" and he/she is transformed into "The Hero." This journey is a labor not of self-discovery, but of self-rediscovery of the divine creative image of "*The One*," the Infinite Self that is hidden within all life's creatures waiting to be known and rendered into life.

The mystical traditions of many established religions such as Hinduism, Islam, Judaism and Christianity suggest the desire for *The One* (God) to "see Itself that it may know Itself" was and is the primal and continued impetus for creation that rendered It into life (i.e., God made the world in his own image.) Every religious system is a temporal-dependent, culturally restrictive, allegorical narrative of this transformative process. It is the narrative of life's heroic journey from darkness into light, from non-being into being, from undifferentiated consciousness into differentiated, self-aware consciousness so that God may know God. This journey is the journey that recapitulates the history of the self-emancipation and self-affirmation of ego consciousness into the "I AM" of fully realized identity as it struggles to free itself from the entropic power of the unconscious. To achieve such a feat, it must hold its own in continuous affirmation and creation against the overwhelming odds of entropy and passive equilibrium of non-being.

Great courage and emotional honesty is demanded of anyone willing to fully live life's heroic story and begin the quest for identity, because to do so means to begin a perilous journey and struggle against unimaginable odds. Such courage enables one to leave the safety of complacency and denial and willingly engage the conscious and unconscious illusions and feelings of fear, guilt, anxiety, loneliness and separateness as they are met along the way. These distressing feelings and illusions are the allegorical demons, dragons and monsters of the shadow world often met along the mythological hero's journey. Avoiding them and continuing the journey is not a possibility. Living authentically with emotional honesty allows one to deeply acknowledge and experience these feelings so they may reveal the source of suffering and the solution to the riddle of identity. This engagement and struggle has been referred to mystically as "going into the fires of initiation" with reference to the mythical phoenix and its transformational ascent from the ashes. It is also mythologically represented by the hero's entry into the cave, the dragon's lair or the witch's castle; the crucifixion, wounding, or descent into the underworld; or as being swallowed by the whale. Scientifically, it is the evolutionary journey of life's continuous creation as it evolves through chaos into ever increasing levels of order, complexity and self-awareness.

For you to answer the question "Who am I?" and begin your quest for identity, you must, like the mythical hero, enter the dragon's lair or shadow world of chaos and death—the womb of the personal and collective unconscious. Entrance is achieved through penetrating, purposeful introspection. Once inside, you will confront the dragon of death, chaos and non-being and will be faced with two choices—to fight the dragon and risk death, or to run in fear. To fight the mythical dragon means to struggle against the static equilibrium of non-being, which is the fundamental source of all fear and anxiety that looms ever present in the underworld of the unconscious. To defeat the dragon is to defeat the tail-swallowing serpent of the uroborus *(Fig. 1-1)*, the mythological symbol of the primal womb of unconsciousness and non-being whose siren call always beckons one back into the deep sleep of unconscious living. Defeating this uroboric dragon is the hero's deed of many mythologies, legends and literature *(Fig. 1-2)*. Through its defeat, you are transformed into a higher state of consciousness and self-realization.[1] This act is self-affirming and transformational, because it reaffirms life and clarifies identity. Although it is mythologically an archetypically male act, all con-

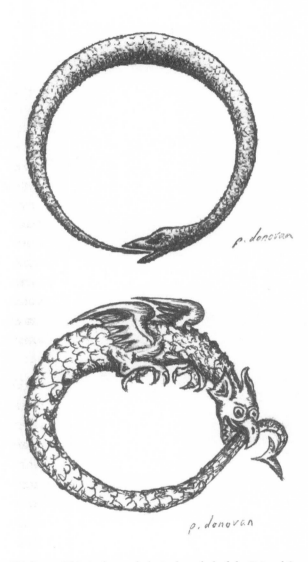

Fig. 1-1. The Uroborus. This is the mythological symbol of the Primal Serpent that is the most ancient deity of the prehistoric world. It appears in the art of ancient Egypt, Mesopotamia, Africa, Mexico, South America, and India. There are pictures of it in Navajo sand paintings and alchemical texts. It is the Alpha and the Omega (the beginning and the end). It devours and yet gives birth to itself. It is the symbol of life in continuous creation and represents the Eternal Womb that has given birth to all.

Fig. 1-2. Pen and ink rendering by P. Donovan of Raphael's painting, St. George and the Dragon. National Gallery of Art, Washington, D.C.

scious, sentient beings, male or female, must experience this heroic act, as all who complete it will win their soul—the female archetype of the self-liberating wellspring of creativity, immortality and contextual identity often referred to as "The Holy Spirit."[2] The irony, however, is that to defeat this uroboric dragon of non-being you must surrender your self to the reality of non-being. You must lose yourself to win yourself. More will be said about this in following chapters.

The courage and personal integrity required to undertake life's heroic journey and achieve such a deed is impressive. The respected, contemporary theologian and philosopher, Paul Tillich, Ph.D., called this requisite valor "the courage to be." In his book by that name, Tillich states, "The courage to be is the ethical act in which man affirms his own being in spite of those elements of his existence which conflict with his essential self-affirmation."[3] However, in the act of affirming one's own being, the elements that conflict with this process are never eliminated. They cannot be eliminated because they are the elements of one's own existence and belong to life itself. They are, instead, *transformed*. They become the fair maiden or virgin that is won, the magical child, the treasure hard to attain, the Holy Grail, the pearl of great price, the elixir of life, etc. All of which are the mystical and mythological representations of this transformational element—the frog who, once kissed, becomes the prince. In truth, they become the self-liberating wellspring of creativity and immortality through which the hero (the male archetype mythologically representing the conscious, egoic self of every individual) is revivified and reborn anew as Thou—the female archetype of the eternal, all-inclusive, Infinite Self.

The passive equilibrium and inertia of non-being—of death—are overcome through the hero's deed, and, by it, the limited, individualized consciousness of the *I* is united with the universal consciousness and contextual identity of the Thou. In other words, through the death of the egoic self, the hero wins his soul, the feminine archetype or Holy Spirit that is the original, eternal and essential self from which *all creative acts* spring forth and through which *all life* is experienced as *Thou*. As psychologist and mythologist Erich Neumann informs us, "The hero myth is fulfilled only when the ego identifies with this self."[4] This situation only occurs "when the personality experiences dying as a simultaneous act of self-reproduction," and the "twofold, finite self is reborn as the total Infinite Self."[5] Through this rebirth or resurrection, you realize your eternal and lasting essence and identity as part of the whole (as God), and move closer to becoming a perfected soul and escaping from the jaws of fate and the flux of instinctive, unconscious living. Through this rebirth, you step upon your path of destiny to rise above the instinctual trappings of the limited self (eat, sleep and procreate) to become the Greater Self that surpasses itself, the self whose self-affirmation, according to Tillich, "is virtue and courage."[6] Through this rebirth you live the mystery of life's story and become the answer to its query.

The elements that resist

The elements that resist the expression of your greater identity appear in the guises of feelings and experiences that threaten you with pain, chaos, death, and non-being. According to Tillich, these elements are, at their very core, rooted in the anxiety of non-being and the fear of death.[7] When you allow your fear and anxiety of these elements to dominate, circumscribe, and sculpt your life on any level, you deny yourself the experience of your "essential affirmation of being," (your eternal and lasting essence and identity). In a sense, you deny yourself the hero's deed. This can happen in varying degrees at any level of your life and when it does, life at that level is then lived disingenuously and passionlessly in a state of existence in conflict with itself. Being then, is not affirmed and the specter of death and non-being looms ever present as the demons and dragons come forth from the caves and underworld of the unconscious as disease in all its various forms to ravage and pillage your mind, body and relationships to a degree correspondent to the depth of your denial. Anxiety-ridden, irresolute impotence and evolutionary paralysis eventually set in from the subconscious tension between unaffirmed being and the threat of non-being. The question of identity goes unanswered, and your potential, unfulfilled and unrealized.

The roots of illness

Through our research for this book, coupled with our years of clinical experience, we have found most people dwell in an existential quandary of identity. This is particularly true for those manifesting signs and symptoms of illness. They are either consciously unaware of their identity crisis or unable to fully live the hero's journey and manifest their true essential nature or essence of being, due to various psycho-emotional traumas that have occurred in their lives. The vital force of life that surges through them and drives the evolution of their consciousness on its sacred quest for identity is then suppressed and distorted within the various levels and aspects of their lives affected by these traumas. As a result, they feel trapped between the fear of being (living their essential nature or essence of being) and the fear of non-being (ego-death and meaninglessness). Caught in the mire of this identity confusion and haunted by the nagging, incessant disquietude of non-being and meaninglessness, they are either unable or unwilling to take the risk of discovering their essential essence and live fully and forthrightly in a manner consistent with who and what they really are. To ease or mitigate the distress of such a situation, they unconsciously rationalize the unimportance of the hero's quest, deny the existence of the dragons, and turn an apathetic, deaf ear to the cries of the fair, young virgin or magical child—their soul. They then submerge themselves in the depthless realm of mind-altering substances and addictions; adult toys; status symbols; the insatiable pursuit of material wealth; and shallow, codependent, and dysfunctional interpersonal relationships absent of any real intimacy and meaning. At the same time, they will begin living their lives vicariously through the mindless melodramas of television sitcoms, the latest Super Bowl, reality TV, and virtual reality computer games. The degree to which they submerge themselves in these distractive and, at times, destructive living habits is directly associated with their degree of denial and/or need to escape the nagging discomfort of life's transformative demands. For some, it can be just a brief, periodic interlude—a periodic "vacation"—and is well balanced with "real living." For others, it can be self-destructive.

This pattern of distracting, pacifying choices is not new to any of us. We are all familiar with such feeble attempts to narcotize and anesthetize ourselves to varying degrees from the disease of unrealized potential and the quiet desperation of unaffirmed being. Such choices, however, rob us of the rich, nourishing experiences of living passionately, intimately, sensually and authentically in the moment and tend only to exacerbate feelings of separateness and isolation. If, in the midst of this situation, we have no sense of connectedness to something greater than ourselves, no knowledge of the laws of causality, or no grand overview of the design of life, we easily succumb to a world ruled by fear and the irrationality of chance. At such a point, the strain of simple, daily existence becomes heavy and oppressive. Exhausted by the strain, while confused, frustrated and disillusioned from the futility of such hollow pursuits, our facade of superficial order crumbles into chaos as a pernicious, paralyzing depression sets in.

In this state of chaos, the dragons of unaffirmed being are freed from their chains of suppression and denial, and emerge as the morbid phenomena of disease (physically, emotionally and psychologically). They rise from the unconscious and, if not confronted and transformed, devastate one's mind and body—one's preconceived notions of what life ought to be. To confront and transform these denizens of the unconscious is to confront and dispel the illusions that have distracted, detained and denied the full expression of your vital force and the evolutionary journey of your consciousness towards self-realization. If, caught in the throes of such a crisis, you are willing to risk death and the uncertainty of change, take up the fight, defeat the illusions of fear and free the virgin maiden—your essential and Infinite Self, illness can become the vehicle for self-affirming, healing transformation.

We believe illness is the evidence of life struggling to defeat and transform the monsters of unconscious illusions and fears and reaffirm itself against the inertia of equilibrium and non-being. In a more personal context, illness is the evidence of your essential Infinite Self, your own true essence of being, struggling to affirm itself against the inertia, complacency and denial of unconscious, uncreative, instinctual living. Ironically, this struggle, often experienced as illness, is also the process of life struggling to grow, transform and evolve. Therefore, as a process of life, *illness should not be eliminated or denied.* It is a heroic journey that should be experienced, passed through and transformed into health. Through illness, you can discover and dissolve the illusions that have denied the full expression of your vital force and essential self-affirmation. Through illness, you can be reborn anew from the limited, exclusive self of *I* into the eternal, all-inclusive self of *Thou.* Through illness you are healed—you are made whole again.

Healing and wholeness

All real healing is transformational and life affirming. All healing, like all illness, "knows only one goal: to make us become whole."[8] It transforms the identity consciousness of the exclusive, individual I, which holds one prisoner to the illusion of separateness, into the inclusive *Thou* consciousness of universal, contextual identity. It is an act of unification and true individual self-affirmation where, as you become I you recognize your beingness in and identity with the whole—with "The Divine." As Jewish mystic and philosopher Martin Beuber exclaims, "*I* become through my relationship to the *Thou*; as *I* become I, I say *Thou.*"[9] The purpose of the hero's journey and the secret of true healing lie within this transformational act.

This concept parallels the thinking of 17th century Jewish philosopher Baruch de Spinoza, considered one of the greatest of modern philosophers, who believed that true individual self-affirmation and, therefore, true healing, is an act of participation in the Divine self-affirmation, in the Divine Whole. He believed that when a soul recognizes itself, it recognizes its inherent beingness in God.[10] *I*, then, is defined through its relationship to *Thou* (the Whole) as a part of the Whole. As you recognize your true essential nature of being *(I)*, you recognize the true essential nature of the whole *(Thou)* of which you are a part and your participation within it. By this act of recognition, according to mystical tradition, the purpose of life is fulfilled (i.e., "God's will to see God" is fulfilled).[11] By this act, the answer to the question "Who/What am I?" becomes self-evident, and the hero's victory is realized. Also, by this act of recognition the mystery of life's story is revealed, healing becomes complete, and the soul cries out ecstatically, "I Am that who I Am," as it claims its unique beingness as an integral part of the universe and reflects that unique beingness back to The Face of God.[12] But essential to this revelational and transformational process is the illusion of separateness.

Chapter 2

The Necessary Illusion of Separateness

"The opposite is beneficial;
from things that differ comes the fairest attunement;
all things are born through strife."

Heraclitus, Greek philosopher,
c. 540–c. 480 B.C.

"The world, harmoniously confused,
Where order in variety we see,
And where, tho' all things differ,
All agree."

Alexander Pope
18th century English poet

The paradox

As some of the more self-aware characters in life's continuing story, we humans experience life as a paradox of singularity and duality, wholeness and fragmentation, unity and separation, self and non-self caught within the tension of being and non-being (life and death). We come into this world at birth, as an individualized life with our own particular characteristics and potentialities given to us by our parents through the unique DNA combination specific only to each one of us. Yet, paradoxically, because that very same DNA is present in all life forms on this planet, we are, at the same time, alike and forever linked to each other and to all life on earth. Also, although we are born a separate individual, we are simultaneously connected and dependent. We are an umbilicated extension of our mother, fully dependent on her for our most basic needs just as we were in her womb. Then, as the umbilical cord is cut, we cry out in passionate rebellion against separation from her, only to struggle later, rebelliously, to finalize that separation during subsequent adolescence and adulthood. So, the dance of life goes on, struggling for individuality while longing for unity with ego consciousness caught between the tension of the two.

Separation and choice in the light of consciousness

No one can ever fully develop into an individual adult (independent, self-actualized, self-motivated, etc.) without an act of separation. Without separation there is no beginning of our story, no birth, no creation of the world, no light from the darkness, no fruit from the tree to carry its seed. The material universe would be "without form, and void" and darkness would be forever "upon the face of the deep" if it were not for an act of separation.[1] Without separation, there would be no mirror through which "God could see God"—there would be nothing![2]

In the creation legends of nearly all peoples and religions, the first act of creation is an act of separation, commonly the separation of the "World Parents"—female and male, earth and heaven—and the separation of order out of chaos. From a Late Sumerian cuneiform creation text of ca. 2000 B.C., we are told that "when 'Heaven-and-Earth' emerged from the primal sea, its form was of a mountain whose summit, Heaven (An), was male and lower portion, Earth (Ki), female. Further, from this dual being the air-god Enlil was born, by whom the two were separated."[3] In the Greek classical myth, Earth (Gaia) is separated from Heaven (Ouranos) by their son Kronos.[4] From the Hindu *Brihadaranyka Unpanishad*, Brahma, the Creator form of Brahman, split his body into two halves, male and female, because of his loneliness and yearning for company.[5]

This process of creation also coincides with, or is marked by, the coming of the light. "And God said, Let there be light: and there was light. And God saw the light, that it was good: and God divided the light from the darkness."[6] This light, according to Neumann, "is the symbol of consciousness and illumination" and is the "prime object of the cosmogonies of all peoples."[7] It is this light of consciousness that, by an act of discrimination, "sunders the world into opposites," for "experience of the world is only possible through opposites."[8] All ego-consciousness caught in the illusion of duality separates and discriminates, as Carl G. Jung informs us, and hence, sunders the world into opposites.[9] To experience the world through opposites is to experience the world consciously through contrast and comparison, both of which ultimately require the cognitive act of choice.

To experience the world consciously
is to experience the world:
Through the *illusion of separateness,*
Through *contrast* and *comparison,*
Through the cognitive act of *choice.*

Choice can only be exercised in the light of consciousness and only through the experience of differences, engendered by the perception of duality and separateness, can there be the possibility of choice. To choose anything, one must first be conscious of the fact that a choice exists and can be made. Then further, one must be aware of the differences between those elements or subjects of the choice. This requires some degree of discrimination by contrasting and comparing those elements. Finally, when this choice is not predetermined or predestined and when it is self-volitional with no precognizance of its outcome, it is free (i.e., free choice). Free choice is exercised by consciousness through uncertainty and risk because the consequences of any choice are never completely knowable. At best, only the probability of any particular consequence or outcome can be known or calculated. Additionally, and most importantly, the ability of consciousness to choose freely under its own volition without any previously known, predetermined outcomes implies free will.

Uncertainties and probabilities are woven into the fabric of the universe. The uncertainty of definite outcomes to any one choice appears to be in concert with the nature of reality at its most primary and fundamental level as described by quantum physics.[10] Heisenberg's "uncertainty principle" tells us that predetermined outcomes are nonexistent because all of the factors influencing a particular event at any one moment in time and space (and all of the factors influencing those factors, *ad infinitum*) can never be known. Even more, if all of the factors were known, the knowing itself (as an added factor) would most likely change the outcome so that it might not be the one previously known. Uncertainties and probabilities are the best anyone can ever hope for when it comes to knowing a definite outcome of any choice before that choice is made. The only way to know for sure is to choose. By choosing, consciousness becomes a self and transforms the quantum, non-local world of probabilities and potentialities into the materialized, local-world of subjective reality.[11] Choice is the chisel with which we sculpt and shape the reality of who and what we are. We are what we are by the choices we make. By the continuous act of choosing, life writes its own story, following the plot of self-realization through self-reflection. By your choices you are known and you write your own character into the story of life. In other words: "You make the bed you lie in," or as Jesus declares in Matthew 7.20, "by their fruits ye shall know them." By their choices ye shall know them.

> By choosing, consciousness becomes a self.
> Choice is the chisel with which we sculpt and
> shape the reality of who and what we are.

Free will (the freedom to choose an action without any preeminent cause, act upon that choice, and then experience the consequences of that action/choice) is very important to the evolution of consciousness and the development of self-identity. It is the prime directive of life. Life evolves and unfolds to become self-aware and realize its full potential and identity through the continuous action of choice and the ever-present risk of pain and non-being associated with the outcomes of that choice. The importance of this is all too obvious when individual freedom is denied or taken away. Many people have sacrificed much, including life, for their freedom to choose and be able to live their lives freely in a manner consistent with who they truly are so that they can realize their full potential.

The 13th century Catholic theologian and scholastic philosopher Thomas Aquinas recognized the theological value and significance of free will with respect to God, especially for humanity. He believed free will "was built into the fabric of the divinely created order" and allowed humanity and all of God's creatures to participate in God's own being, each according to his/her own nature and essence.[12] He further believed, through the autonomy allowed by free will, each one of us could *freely* love God *by our own choice* and *freely* return to God as the Source of All.

In light of this information (considering the many paradise stories associated with the creation myths of the world), one might see "The Fall" from Paradise as necessary, particularly regarding the Biblical story of Genesis.[13] (The original sin of the Fall was celebrated as a blessed sin "O felix culpa!" "Oh blessed sin!" in the Eastern liturgy of the Catholic Church.) In that story, the fall from paradise catalyzed the development of individualized self-consciousness because *it made choice possible.* The Fall occurred after the archetypal male and female potential of individualized self-consciousness (Adam and Eve) were faced with the choice of eating or not eating the apple from the tree of the "dark knowledge of good and evil." By choosing to eat the apple they acquired the knowledge of good and evil, which is the knowledge of polarity and maximal contrast essential to the illusion of separateness. That knowledge transformed their potential into the manifest reality of individualized *I*-ness; banished them from the paradisal world of integrated wholeness and unindividuated consciousness of *The All* (the Garden of Eden); and forced them to enter the illusory world of polarity and separateness. Their action "condemned" them to a life of choice with its subsequent consequences and risks.[14] This "fall" symbolizes the stepping forth of the exclusive, individualized "I" of self-aware consciousness from the paradisal state of universal, *non*-self-aware consciousness where there is no "*I*-ness," only the total Oneness of The All. This marked the beginning of the hero's journey for consciousness as its individuated, egoic expression was birthed from its uroboric womb of unindividuated non-being. With this act of separation came the experience of pain and suffering associated with isolation, loneliness, the uncertainty of choice and the ever present, possibility of non-being—of death. With it also came the desperate longing for unity and wholeness. This is the longing that has become an integral part of the very fabric and essence of individuated, self-aware consciousness since the moment it separated from the unity and wholeness of the paradisal state — the longing for home.

Theologians call this longing the "original guilt" from the "Original Sin" of the Fall. It is the "guilt" felt by the egoic self because of its separation from the paradisal womb of unindividu-ated consciousness to individuate and create the mirror of self-reflection through which consciousness perceives itself and realizes its identity. This loss of wholeness and of total unconscious integration with The Source "is experienced as the primary loss; it is the original deprivation which occurs at the very outset of the ego's evolution."[15] It is the pain we all carry in those empty spaces of our aloneness, the one we face in "the dark night of the soul."

We prefer not to refer to this feeling of pain and loss as guilt (as do Judeo-Christian beliefs) because guilt implies a judgment of wrong action (i.e., "original sin.") We believe this act of separation was neither right nor wrong; it was and continues to be simply an act of creation necessary for and integral to the evolution of self-aware consciousness. On the other hand, it did bring about an unnatural or illusory state of separateness and fragmentation. As consciousness participates in that illusion, it carries the memory of the more *real* or natural state of wholeness or integration with *The All* and sometimes experiences the longing to be forgiven back into that state of oneness as guilt.

Identity through maximal contrast and polarity

The separation of light from darkness or order from chaos, and the opposition between them, represents the primal movement from singularity to duality and eventually to multiplicity. Most importantly, it represents the creative principle of "maximal contrast."[16] In other words, without darkness to define and contrast it, there would be no light; without the possibility of non-being, there would be no being; without the possibility of chaos there would be no order. In Taoism, maximal contrast is modeled by the Yin-Yang symbol.*(Fig. 2-1)* The most elegant examples of maximal contrast in the world of form and living systems are the contrasts between inside and outside, order and chaos, and symmetry and asymmetry.[17] In biological systems, a boundary (such as the cell membrane) or an act of severance or discrimination distinguishes inside from outside, order from chaos, but most importantly, self from non-self. On the inside is self (that which is known or familiar) while on the outside is nonself (that which is unknown and unfamiliar). The inside also represents order and symmetry, while the outside represents chaos and asymmetry.

The action of separation or discrimination, which sets the boundaries between inside and outside, is just that—an action, a dynamic process. This action or "process" requires a "thing" to act upon and introduces another aspect of maximal contrast—*process* and *thing*. This is best illustrated linguistically by the relationship of a verb (process) to its noun (thing). In physics, this contrast could be represented in the wave/particle duality relationship (wave is process and particle is thing) while in living systems it is experienced as the germination/seed, growth/organism or mind/body relationship. Theologically it represents the opposition of heaven to earth and "spirit" to "flesh." In the world of form, it can also be seen as the relationship between asymmetry and symmetry respectfully. Archetypally, "asymmetry can be represented by a dynamic form that continuously breaks symmetries as it unfurls" or undergoes its process while symmetry can be represented "by the most compact structural forms (in any given dimension)" such as the sphere and the five Platonic solids (tetrahedron, cube, octahedron, cube icosahedron, dodecahedron)[18] *(Fig. 2-2)*. These are static,

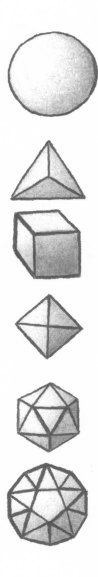

Fig. 2-1. Yin-Yang symbol.

*Fig. 2-2. Sphere with the
Five Platonic Solids*

crystalized forms—things—that are not continuously undergoing dynamic fludic change.

As a general rule relative to living systems, the asymmetry of the dynamic unfolding process is conceptually inside, contained by its symmetrical projective complement (its container) as DNA is contained inside the cell nucleus or the seed inside its fruit-pod or shell. But, inside becomes outside and outside becomes inside as the unfolding process of continuous creation develops. We will address this more specifically in the following chapters.

Examples of the Maximal Contrast of Process and Thing

Process	Thing
Verb	Noun
Wave	Particle
Germination	Seed
Growth/Development	Living Organism
Relationship	Objects
Asymmetry	Symmetry
Mind	Body
Consciousness	Structure

The universe was formed and the world was ordered from the primary principle of definition through opposition and maximal contrast established by the first separation of order from chaos, light from darkness. This act of discrimination ordered the world and made the development of spatial orientation and the setting of boundaries possible.[19] It also made the development of self-awareness and self-consciousness possible by allowing the maximal contrast of inside and outside. Through this contrast an internal, subjective experience of the outside world (selfness of I) is realized.

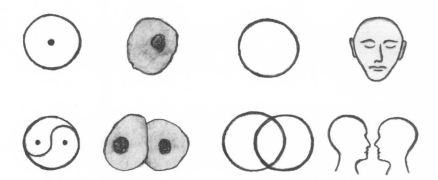

Fig. 2-3. The Monad and the Dyad. Top row: The monad as seed-point, single cell, circle and face. Bottom row: The monad in relationship as the dyad — yin-yang, the two-cell stage after division, two circles in relationship forming the vesica pisces, "The Face" reflecting "The Face." From the relationship of the two the universe is born.

Oscillation from maximal contrast

Space comes into existence by separation and maximal contrast. All spatial relationships begin from two points—x and y. From this polarity and contrast, the dyad (with its two opposing points in spatial relationship to each other) is created from the monad. This primary act in the creative process is clearly evident and best modeled in cellular division and replication. In preparation for division, intracellular DNA polarizes within the cell. The cell then divides and a new boundary is established via the cell membrane and the one becomes two *(Fig. 2-3)*. From the two, the many are born and a whole organism is created—a community of individuals working together as one.

The dyad infers a spatial relationship and from it, the spatial prerequisite for the motion of oscillation is established. Oscillation is the rhythmic movement back and forth between two poles or points of maximal contrast. It is the motion that gives birth to the "rhythm of life." It makes vibration and the quantum wave phenomenon possible, hence, from it light is born and energy and matter are created. Through the rhythmic vibration and movement of oscillation made possible by maximal contrast, the infinite breath and pulse of life streams forth and "the Word is made manifest." Through it also the resonant vibrational patterns of the tiny strings of matter that determine the microcosmic origins of particle masses and force charges in the universe are made possible.[20] Most importantly, however, oscillation engenders the movement of giving and receiving, which ultimately transforms the dyad of polarity into the monad of oneness again through sharing and relationship. Through relationship the two are made one as the face of each is reflected in the other. Through relationship also, *The One* is maintained in *The Many*.

From the spatial relationship of the diad, the "space between" is established. The space between is the "Holy of Holies" where the two become as one. It is the place of relationship where The Lover and The Beloved meet on the wedding bed of profound relatedness. It is also the place where "The Mirror of Existence" was placed by The Divine One so that the *The One* could see Itself in the Face of The Many and vice versa.

Polarity and attraction

Polarity is another feature of maximal contrast. It is essential for the formation and structure of all matter. As the polar charge of positive and negative, it determines the electrical characteristics of subatomic particles (protons, electrons), atoms and molecules, and effects the forces that govern their behavior. As male and female, it determines the relationship that generates life. Without polarity there would be no electromagnetic attraction, no glue to hold the fundamental particles of matter together and no energy to form and shape them into existence. Without polarity there would be no germination of life, no light, no universe!

Self-consciousness and awareness of "the other"

The development of self-consciousness and identity is wholly dependent upon an act of severance giving way to maximal contrast and the illusion of separateness. In fact, consciousness may be essentially defined as *an awareness of separateness.* The formation of consciousness and self-identity goes hand in hand with the fragmentation of the world continuum into separate objects and parts that can be contrasted, compared and ultimately, "related to."[21] For instance, for consciousness to perceive itself (for God to see God), "it must first cut itself up into at least one state which sees, and at least one other state which is seen."[22] The great mystic and Kabbalistic teacher of the *Zohar*, Rabbi Simeon, taught that humans would be neutral, ignorant beings unable to distinguish and contrast things essential to mental growth and spiritual development and progress if God did not separate light from darkness, good from evil, giving from taking.[23]

To compare and contrast, to discriminate, to distinguish and mark off—these are all acts of consciousness and require an awareness of opposites and separate things, an awareness of inside (self) and outside (non-self). David Chalmers, Ph.D., Associate Professor of Philosophy at the University of California, Santa Cruz, suggests that awareness and consciousness are coexistent, possibly the same.[24] Considering these facts, we suggest the development of self-aware consciousness is contingent upon awareness of separateness and maximal contrast. Such awareness leads to the experience of inside and outside, me and you or "self" and "non-self" respectively and establishes the prerequisite for an internal, subjective experience of self. By the perceptions created from self cognitively contrasting and comparing itself with the non-self of the outside world, a relationship is established between self and nonself. The internal experience of self is then subjectively realized through its relationship to the external world of non-self and the sensations produced by that relationship. Physicist Amit Goswami theorizes that the universe could not become self-aware without this relationship, without the "immanent world of manifestation" (the material world). By the universe manifesting itself materially as matter, it allows its self to experience itself as separate from the object it perceives.[25]

Defining consciousness

Consciousness is a process, not a thing, and cannot be defined or understood as a thing. According to philosopher Christian de Quincy, Professor of Cosmology and Consciousness at John F. Kennedy University, "consciousness, as process, informs matter."[26] But of what does it inform matter? We suggest it informs matter of a very simple and primal pattern of activity, that of a *reiterative, self-reflective cycle.* This is the cyclic pattern of outside continuously becoming inside and inside continuously becoming outside. The outside world of *non-self* is ingested by the inside world of *potential-self* where it is digested, assimilated and experienced as the internalized, subjective reality of *self.* This internal reality is then projected outward to the outside world to affect the outside world and then be reingested, and so on. In other words, the inside experiences the internal reality as self through the *sensations* engendered by the outside world. These sensations are then interpreted as *perceptions* by this self. Those perceptions are then projected to the outside world. This may well be the continuous pattern of activity or nature of consciousness that leads to self-awareness. By this action, the inside world of self experiences itself as distinct from the outside world of non-self, thus allowing for the continued illusion of self as a separate reality.

The initial act of separation that "divided the light from the darkness" and allowed *The One* to become *The Many* may have been this primal, self-reflective act of consciousness that initially informed and continues to inform matter of the recurring, self-reflective theme of life's continuing story. This act was an act of self-affirmation and beingness that initially occurred when the eternal singularity first condensed its "selfness" out of the Universal Womb of non-being into the seed-point of self, and then projected its "selfness" out into the emptiness of non-being for the purpose of self-realization.

Consciousness:

- Consciousness is the *process that informs matter.* It is not a "thing." It cannot be defined or understood as a thing.

- Consciousness, *as process,* informs matter of the reiterative, self-reflective cyclic pattern of outside continuously becoming inside and inside continuously becoming outside. The outside world of *non-self* is ingested by the inside world of *potential-self* where it is digested, assimilated and experienced through sensation as the internalized, subjective reality of self. This internal reality is then projected outward to affect the outside world and then be re-ingested *ad infinitum.*

- Self-consciousness is contingent upon *awareness of separateness* and the maximal contrast of inside and outside.

- Self-consciousness occurs as the inside world of self perceives itself as distinct from the outside world of non-self allowing for the continued illusion of self as a separate reality.

Relationship and identity

The continued awareness of self as a separate reality is an illusion caused by the state of separation and maximal contrast. This illusion is necessary, however, for the development of relationship. Whenever there are two or more of anything, there exists a relationship between them. Through the self-reflective phenomenon inherent in relationship, individual identity is revealed. Ironically, however, it is also through relationship that the illusion of separateness is eventually transcended and the separate *I* is realized as a part of the greater *whole*. Through relationship the reality of "The Whole" is maintained and a person becomes part of a higher and qualitatively different identity, that of unity.[27] Martin Buber addresses this when he states, "The man who emerges from the act of pure relation that so involves his being has now in his being something more that has grown in him, of which he did not know before…."[28] That "something" is not only the realization of one's separate or individual identity, but also the realization of one's contextual identity as part of the whole—one's true identity. This realization, however, demands of one's mind the ability to hold two conflicting or paradoxical concepts simultaneously in conscious thought (i.e., wholeness and part or unity and separateness). It demands of one the realization of that great mystery, expressed in the Hindu Upanishads, which is the mystery of all being: *"Tat tvan asi."* ("Thou art that," or "You yourself are It!")[29] This feat is quite difficult for the human psyche to do since it has been formed and shaped by cultural conditioning for millennia to the illusion of duality and fragmentation instead of unity and wholeness. A thing is either "this" or "that," a separate part or a whole, but not both at the same time.

Upon being born, you are recognized as part of the family in which you serve as an individual thread of the fabric of the most primal web or network of relationships. For the rest of your life, you will be a character in the paradoxical melodrama of *separateness* and *unity*, of *me* and *us*, *I* and *Thou*. You will strive to develop your own individual identity, to find your "own world by seeing and hearing and touching and shaping it," while at the same time struggling continuously to be gently enraptured into satisfying relationships and a sense of unity through the bonds of love.[30] The underlying motivation for this effort is self-realization through the illuminating experience of self in relation to others. As Buber reminds us, "all real living is meeting."[31] All real living is relating.

The greatest human need, after the basic survival needs have been met, according to the respected American psychologist Abraham Maslow, is the need to know who you are at the deepest spiritual level (i.e., the need for self-realization, self-actualization and self-affirmation).[32] Fulfillment of this need requires the existential paradox of experiencing yourself simultaneously as whole and part—as a separate individual and as part of a greater whole (marriage, family, tribe, clan, community, etc.). Through the reflection of your being in the eyes of "the other," you behold your essential nature, as well as your contextual nature as part of a larger communal self. This is only a micro-personalized experience of the grander experience of "God beholding God." As "God beholds God," God realizes God's essential individual nature of being and is made whole again through that realization (although God is always whole).[33] Hence, the reason for creation: to establish the phenomenon of relationship through the illusion of separateness so that "God could see God."

Vesica pisces as the doorway of life

Relationship is born from the illusion of separateness and the duality of maximal contrast, and relationship makes reflection possible. Mystical traditions teach that reflection of *The One* in the face of *The Many* is the reason *The One* becomes *The Many* so that God could see God. The dyad is the doorway for this process. The dyad, represented geometrically and symbolically as two facing spheres (three dimensions) or two linked circles (two dimensions) in reflective relationship, presents this lesson geometrically. The orifice formed by the two interpenetrating spheres or circles when the center of each lies on the circumference of the other is the "vesica pisces" or "vessel of the fish." *(Fig. 2-4)* It rep-

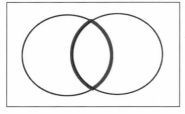

Fig. 2-4. The "vesica pisces" is the orifice formed by the two interpenetrating spheres or circles when the center of each lies on the circumference of the other. It is the symbol of the two in relationship forming the doorway of creation.

resents the *sacred space* where the *two meet as one* in relationship. It is the "doorway of creation" established by the reflective, procreative relationship of profound relatedness through which all life realizes its beingness. Sex is the biological insurance policy programmed into living systems to guarantee this relationship, and the vesica pisces is the altar of the courtship bed upon which it is executed.

The vesica pisces is one of the simplest and most informative geometrical and archetypal symbols known.[34] "It is the womb from which are generated all the numbers and ratios of the sacred Temple" and of all temples of antiquity.[35] It appears in the sacred temples of Egypt as a repetitive shape which may represent the field pattern of "the void." *(Fig. 2-5)* The Christian symbol of the fish is created from a vesica pisces *(Fig. 2-6)*. The vesica pisces is well-known in art, mathematics, geometry, architecture, mythology and theology as an archetype of symmetry and was depicted in the sacred art of the earliest of civilizations. As one of the most ancient of symbols, it has historically represented the fusion of the two worlds of spirit and matter.[36] More contemporarily, it may be perceived as a symbol of the sacred marriage of the formless, transcendent, nonlocal world of quantum potentialities (the "hidden domain") penetrating the local world of matter.[37] It is the abode of the *I* where the experience of conscious observation collapses the domain of quantum wave potential into particle reality and "makes a causal pathway in the fabric of possibilities."[38] It is the symbol of the "wave form" in physics and may be the geometric shape through which light was created. *(Fig. 2-7)* Mathematician

Fig. 2-5. Left: This may be the <u>best</u> representation of what the primal, spatial field looks like in our limited conception. From this pattern, all geometric constructs can be made from which all form can arise.

Below: It is based on a fundamental pattern of intersecting circles or spheres forming multiple vesica pisces. It is an ancient and sacred pattern.

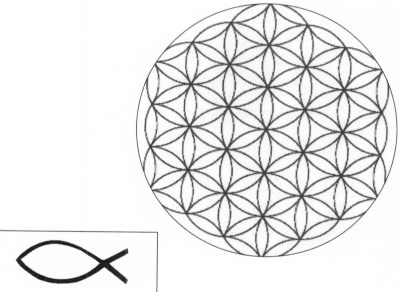

Fig. 2-6.

Fig. 2-7. Wave form.

Michael Schneider describes it as "the crucible of the creating process. It is an opening to the womb from which geometric forms are born. It brings forth shapes and patterns from the archetypal world of ideal geometry."[39]

The vesica pisces is commonly referred to as a "womb" or "doorway" through which pattern and form are born into the material world. The corpus callosum (the network of nerve fibers in the central portion of the brain interconnecting the right and left hemispheres) neurologically functions as a vescica pisces. It acts as the "doorway" between the right and left hemispheres of the brain through which abstract thought and concepts are realized into the rational world and brought to fruition. (The right hemisphere is where pattern recognition and abstract thought takes place [process] and the left hemisphere is where practical, rational thought takes place [thing].) The vesica pisces is also represented biologically as the female genitalia (vulva) because of its shape and function as a birthing doorway into the world of form *(Fig. 2-8)*. In Sanskrit, the name of the vesica pisces is the term for the female generative organs.

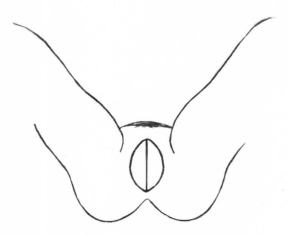

Fig. 2-8. The vesica pisces as the female vulva

The gravity of love

The Many are born through the polar relationship of the two—male and female, positive and negative, spirit and matter, yin and yang, lover and beloved. That which draws and holds them into relationship is their inherent desire to be one, to merge into unity again and be whole. This mergence and unification with "the other," forms a *Thou*—a whole. *I* is expanded and strengthened as it becomes *Thou*. The self is extended and magnified through the union and a greater identity is realized, i.e., the identity of the whole. As scientific observation of biological systems has revealed, a greater assurance of individual and species survival occurs when individuals come together in cooperation to form a community.

Love is the force that unites and draws every individual I into relationship, every part into a whole. It is the gravitational pull of *Thou* upon an *I*—of the Divine Singularity of unity and wholeness upon *the many*. Through the experience of love, the illusion of separateness is dissolved and the reality of oneness is realized. *Love is the two seeking to be one again*. Through love, opposites are reconciled. Through love, the mystic's mind is capable of simultaneously holding two paradoxical and apparently opposing concepts in conscious thought long enough to be able to realize The Whole: *tat tvan asi*, "I am that!" As the great mythologist Joseph Campbell informs us:

> The ultimate experience of love is a realization that beneath the illusion of two-ness dwells identity: "each is both." This realization can expand into a discovery that beneath the multitudinous individualities of the whole surrounding universe—human, animal, vegetable, even mineral—dwells identity; whereupon the love experience becomes cosmic, and the beloved who first opened the vision is magnified as the mirror of creation.[40]

The great mystic and Sufi poet Rumi addresses this same idea in his poem, "When A Man And A Woman Become One" (*Excerpted from "When a Man and a Woman Become One," from* Love Is a Stranger. Selected Lyric Poetry of Jelaluddin Rumi, *Helminski K [Trans]*):

Be fair, You who are the Glory of the just.
You, Soul, free of "we" and "I",
subtle spirit within each man and woman.

When a man and a woman become one,
That "one" is You.
And when that one is obliterated, there You are.

Where is this "we" and this "I"?
By the side of the Beloved.
You made this "we" and this "I"
In order that you might play

This game of courtship with Yourself,
That all "you's" and "I's" might become one soul
And finally drown in the Beloved.[41]

However, even in the unity and oneness of loving, the necessary illusion of separateness must be respected or else identity is lost. Kahlil Gibran, beautifully and poetically describes this in his writing on Marriage (*Excerpted from "Marriage" from* The Prophet *by Kahil Gibran*):

Let there be spaces in your togetherness,
And let the winds of the heavens dance
    between you.
Love one another, but make not a bond of love:
Let it rather be a moving sea between the
    shores of your souls.
Fill each other's cup but drink not from one
    cup.
Give one another of your bread but eat not
    from the same loaf.
Sing and dance together and be joyous, but let
    each one of you be alone,
Even as the strings of a lute are alone though
    they quiver with the same music.
Give your hearts, but not into each other's
    keeping.
For only the hand of Life can contain your
    hearts.
And stand together yet not too near together:
For the pillars of the temple stand apart,
And the oak tree and the cypress grow not in
    each other's shadow.[42]

The *I* must remain an *I* so that it may experience and reflect the *Thou*. The *I* must, as Buber states, "step forth from its singleness to confront the *Thou*."[43]

As we ponder it, the essential truth of it becomes clear. Identity is established and magnified through the reflective nature of relationship and there cannot be relationship without maximal contrast and the perceived experience of duality and separateness. The transformational experience of the two becoming one through love is made possible only by the perception of separateness. This is the quintessential principle for the establishment of identity through self-awareness and the reason for creation and life's diversity. The more diverse life is (the more each individual expresses their own particular characteristics), the greater the potential is for relationship, and hence, the *sacredness of diversity*. To enter into relationship with itself is why *The One* becomes *the many* even though, as St. Symeon states, "the One who has become the many, remains the One undivided."[44] God is known through relationship.

Everything that exists is defined by its relationship to another. Being cannot exist or be fully experienced without the possibility of non-being. Light cannot be recognized as light without the contrast of darkness. Consequently, as stated in Chapter One, the elements that conflict with self-affirmation must never be eliminated because they "belong to existence themselves." As Tillich states, "Being 'embraces' itself and non-being."[45] Consciousness, as the light of being, has the dark sleep of non-being eternally present within it, and this darkness is eternally overcome and transformed in the process of the divine self-affirmation. After all, when light comes into existence by any means, isn't it the light that overcomes the darkness and not the contrary?

It appears that the experience of separation is a necessary illusion for the development of individual identity and self-consciousness. But when this experience is not counterbalanced with a relationship of love and acceptance and the buffering effect of a visceral sense of connectedness and oneness with all things, a high price is extracted.

Chapter 3

Me Against the World

"Everybody's shouting, 'Which side are you on?'"

Bob Dylan, 1941–

In tune with the rhythms of life

The primordial human experience on this planet was deeply immersed in nature. Through the life-supporting activities of hunting and foraging, planting and harvesting, an individual's personal experience was inextricably entwined with those animals and plants that sustained his/her life, and often times, threatened it. Both individual and tribal experiences and behavior were governed by the cycles of sun, moon, and seasons. By these cycles, an individual and the tribal community were continually reminded of the eternal rhythm and relationship of the natural order of things. They witnessed and participated in the act of life feeding upon life to sustain itself; the death of one thing (plant, animal, human) providing sustenance for the life of another. Their intimate relationship with the pulse of the natural world allowed them a subjective sense of oneness with all that is. In that state of awareness, they perceived everything as part of, and inseparable from, everything else (each an extension of the other). In that state also, their illusion of separateness was not nurtured or accentuated to any great degree. Their collective ideas prevailed and group or tribal consciousness was paramount; "our" was the primary self-referential word as opposed to "my." In such a state of consciousness, "the ego was not an autonomous, individualized entity with a knowledge, morality, volition, and activity of its own; it functioned solely as part of the group, and the group with its superordinate power was the only real subject."[1] In these early Neolithic tribal societies, the individual's conscious and unconscious worlds were interfused; his/her individual life experience was merged with the experience of the tribe to the point where the psychological boundaries between self and non-self blurred.

There is substantial anthropological evidence suggesting primordial societies worshiped the feminine qualities of God (the "Mother Goddess") and the life-generating, nurturing powers of nature.[2] In these primordial societies, relationship among all things within the universe was primal. As Joseph Campbell states, people comprehended instinctively the Mother Goddess as "the personification of the energies of nature and life that transform past into future, semen into child, seed into plant."[3] Because of their reverence for the inextricable interconnectedness of all life, they were prone to work cooperatively for the common good of all members of the immediate tribal community and the preservation of the natural resources that nourished their way of life. They often practiced common stewardship of the land and other principal means of production. They shared responsibility for the completion of necessary tasks and shared pleasure in reaping the harvest of their labor. The individual belonged to and was identified by his/her relationship to "the whole." The members of the tribe were equally involved (male and female) in sustaining the integrity and life of the whole community. In turn, the tribe sustained each member and provided each a sense of meaning and purpose.

According to many anthropologists, there was little evidence in these early societies of hierarchy by domination and intimidation where a single individual or group of individuals was allowed to dominate the others of the tribe by force or the implied threat of force to the detriment of the tribe. What hierarchies existed, were more commonly *actualization hierarchies.* These hierarchies are dependant upon divisions of labor and tasks that serve the tribe's best interest and function to maximize the tribe's potential.[4]

This early tribal and communal time in human history may be what has been referred to as "the dream time" by some aboriginal cultures because at this time, the individual ego consciousness had not yet completed its evolution towards autonomy and individualized identity. It had yet to disentangle itself from the unconscious, the group and, eventually, the realm of nature, just as an individual must separate from parents and family in order to develop "a life of his or her own" and become "one's own person." This disentanglement had to happen so that the full realization of individualized consciousness as *I* could come about, and the ego is the vehicle of that expression.

The evolution of "me"

Over the past five to ten thousand years, humanity has slowly completed its disentanglement with the unconscious and the female archetypal world of the realm of nature. This disentanglement reached a zenith in Western Civilization with the Judeo-Christian, patriarchal world view in which nature is perceived as corrupt, "inherently prone to the demonic and responsible for man's fall and continued corruption."[5] The whole sense of the Fall is that nature is corrupt. This change of consciousness has brought about a decline of the agrarian, female-focused, partnership cultures and the advent of the predatory, male-dominant, patriarchal civilization.[6] It also set the stage for the evolution of individuated ego consciousness since ego consciousness is mythologically associated with the male archetype.

Once disengaged from tribal consciousness, the individuated ego-mind tends to fall deeply into the illusion of separateness. An individual's sense of oneness with nature and the tribe is replaced by feelings of isolation and loneliness. The willingness to contribute to communal endeavors for the common good and to share the harvest equally with others in the tribe is supplanted by the need to compete aggressively for survival. Reverence, awe, appreciation, and patience born of faith in the tribal community, the bounty of nature, and the generous beneficence of the Earth-Mother are traded for an anxious, assertive need to dominate nature and force her to escalate productivity to meet the ever-growing material demands of the ego-mind. One's willingness to be merely one member of the extended tribal family is supplanted by the need for ego-aggrandizement via imposed hierarchies of power and control, material acquisition, personal adornment, and other means of elevating oneself above others.

Human consciousness, progressively influenced by the pressures of population expansion, religious fundamentalism, and advances in metallurgy, scientific rationalism, and the technological demands of industrialization, has been overwhelmed with the illusion of separateness. Dualism and separateness have been the cultural story of Western Civilization. As a result, humanity has begun focusing exclusively on the *I* and *my* while the *Thou* and *our* has receded into the background of thought. For those who use technology to hide from the authenticity of deep intimacy and emotional honesty, the facts of life governing human relationships have become the "FAX of life" in a world of "e-male" dominance caught in "the web" of sterilized intimacy. "Things" and outcomes have become more important than process and relationship. Due to society's growing fascination with things, Thou has been replaced by "it." We humans have begun sacrificing the depth and warm embrace of *I-Thou* relationships for the superficial, cold sterility of *me-it* relationships.

Under this illusory perception of me-it, other human beings are seen as objects that can be bought and sold, manipulated or eliminated as one buys and sells goods or discards a cigarette lighter after it has been used. The history of slavery in Western Civilization (Ancient Greece, the Roman Empire, United States of America, to name a few.) is an excellent example of this. A particularly egregious expression of this mindset is found in the infamous Dred Scott Decision written by U.S. Supreme Court Chief Justice, Roger B. Taney.[7] Dred Scott, a Negro man perceived as inferior to the white European, was considered "an ordinary article of merchandise" and was denied his freedom by the U.S. Supreme Court.

This illusory separateness of *I* and *my*, without the counterbalancing realization of *Thou* and *our* with its buffering visceral sense of connectedness and oneness with all things, has engendered feelings of isolation, anxiety, and vulnerability. Such feelings have fostered a pervasive defensive attitude of "me against the world." Everything that is not "me" or "mine" becomes threatening as "the other." All human relationships played out with such an undercurrent of antagonism can only produce conflict and resistance, rather than harmony. All conflicts and wars begin with the word *my* (my country, my religion, my land, my political party, and so forth) while all conflict resolution begins with *our*.

This hostile attitude of "me vs. you" or "us vs. them" is characteristic of the patriarchal "domination" model of civilization pushed to its extreme. At such an extreme, it becomes the diametric opposite of a balanced "partnership" model that engenders integration and cooperation.[8] Driven by the momentum of life's unfolding, the pendulum of ego-consciousness swung too far in the opposite direction in its attempt to disentangle itself from the group and the unconscious realm of the Great Mother to establish autonomy and its own individualized identity.

According to Riane Eisler, the dissemination of the patriarchal model of dominance was intimately associated with the conquering and subjugation of the more peaceful, cooperation-oriented, agrarian Neolithic cultures of Europe and the Near East by aggressive nomadic peoples of Northern Europe and Asia five to ten thousand years ago.[9] The invading nomads were warriors and herdsmen of livestock who worshipped male gods of war, ministered by authoritarian male priesthoods that imposed their interpretation of the will of these gods upon the masses. Well-demarcated, *domination hierarchies* of power relationships (as opposed to actualization hierarchies) were maintained via stratified divisions among the people. This social structure served as an efficient means to control human behavior, and, thereby, perpetuate the existing social order to the advantage of the power elite at the top of the oligarchic pyramid. Domination hierarchies were strictly enforced by intimidation as "all [domination] hierarchies are maintained with the threat of violence."[10]

The individual human being living in such a hostile atmosphere was typically caught in the jaws of an inescapable hierarchical vice comprised of the two foci of power within such a society. In the coldly incisive language of objectivist philosopher and writer Ayn Rand, the average person was trapped between "Attila" and the "witch doctor," between the king and the priesthood, between those who would enslave the body and those who would enslave the mind. An individual challenging either of these power institutions would certainly face annihilation. Favoring either of these often-antagonistic forces would have invited the wrath of the other. Such was the anxiety-charged atmosphere of life for anyone living under the mantle of patriarchal extremism.

The pervasive posture of antagonism and confrontation of the patriarchal extremist model was projected, not merely toward other people, but eventually was directed toward the forces of nature. But natural phenomena were more frightening and could not be as easily controlled as human beings. Nature, as the epitome of the female archetype, always presented the threatening specter of the unconscious realm and the possibility of annihilation and non-being to the patriarchal dominant, male archetype of ego. Thus, in the minds of those living the extreme patriarchal paradigm, nature was not merely an irritating inconvenience and instrument of justice for capricious gods. It was also the courier and executioner of the people's deepest, darkest fear—the fear of death—propelling them back into the womb of the unconscious realm and its looming non-being. As technological advances progressed and the individual ego-mind became powerful enough to suppress (at least temporarily) the unconscious, it could accomplish conscious disengagement from nature and the rest of humanity. As it did so, the ego-mind endeavored to subdue to the service and will of the male archetype, nature and all representations of the female archetype—the womb of the unconscious—including women and all images of and references to the Goddess in culture, myth, and religion. Every individual plays out this "cutting off" or disentanglement from "the mother" as he/she struggles to attain individuality and autonomy. This is particularly true in the teenage years, as any parent who has raised a child through those years will attest to.

This model of human behavior and consciousness that encourages its adherents to suppress all sense of connectedness between *I* and *Thou*, with its primary self-referential word being *my* instead of *our* is, consequently, a model of human behavior without compassion. Compassion comes from a sense of connection and oneness with another. Although it has come to be defined in modern parlance in terms of pity, the Latin derivation of this word arises from roots meaning "suffering together," implying a sharing of feelings and experience, as connoted by the word "empathy." All compassion arises from the word "our." Without this bridling influence on human consciousness, the ego-mind, with its instrument of wanton intellect, is left unchecked in the human psyche. Lacking the moral, ethical, and spiritual guidance of love and compassion, the ego-mind, through intellectual rationalizations, can justify any act that assuages its fears or aggrandizes its artificially inflated, non-contextual sense of itself. For the feminine principle of nature and the female archetype, it is the most dangerous thing in the world. The thousands of women brutally executed by the Catholic Church in the Middle Ages for "practicing witchcraft" will attest to this, as will the thousands more raped, abused, murdered, or veiled and denied their human rights over the ages. The pages of recorded history are soiled with the bloodlust, waste, and horror inflicted upon humanity by power-crazed patriarchal extremist individuals, institutions and societies.

Perhaps the society that most exemplified the horrors of this unbalanced state of consciousness in modern times was Nazi Germany. All the characteristics of patriarchal extremism and unbridled ego were there: the rigid male hierarchy maintained by intimidation and violence, the attitude of "us against the world," the heartlessly brutal extermination of all perceived enemies of the state, the demanded loyalty to a dominant male figure (Der Führer) and the masculine German state (the Fatherland), and the subjugation of all neighboring peoples perceived as weaker, inferior, and easily coercible to the will of the Third Reich.

A more recent and familiar example is the violence and "terrorism" unleashed upon our modern world by patriarchal extremists under the guise of religious fundamentalism. Such egocentric fundamentalism, be it Islamic, Christian, Jewish, or any other, encourages exclusivism and the delusionary belief that "Only we have The Truth and the right moral code for the world because we are 'The Chosen of God.' With God on our side, 'all who are not with us are against us' and therefore, all acts of intimidation and violence against the 'nonbelievers,' the 'infidels' or the 'evil ones' are justified to purge the world of evil and preserve God's morality and peace as we see it." Ironically, this recent terrorism has engendered an equally fundamentalistic and exclusivistic political response from the modern world in the guise of neoconservative imperialism. This patriarchal extremist worldview, perpetuated by fear, has promoted torture and preemptive "first strike" militarism against any persons, country or political/religious group appearing as a threat to its conservative moral and political agenda and convictions. Where is the Right to Life Movement in this situation, or is torture and killing of the "nonbelievers" to assure world peace and morality justified when it is "them" and not "us" who are being tortured and killed?

In the absence of compassion and the counter-balancing feeling of *"other" as part of "self,"* the illusion of separateness, with its consequent antagonistic attitudes of "me versus you," or "us versus them," has contributed mightily to patterns of militaristic, religious and political domination that have plagued humankind for eons. The ubiquitous tendency to dissociate from a sense of responsibility for the consequences of our choices due to our cultural story of exclusivism has allowed the extreme patriarchal ego-mind to engage in an insidious form of self-delusion that has wreaked havoc on humanity and the planet. This mindset allows us to justify hideous acts because we fail to realize our unity with all things. Anything standing in the way of the ego-mind's idealized objective, and the intellect's scheme to reach it, must be eliminated, regardless of whether the obstacle is human, animal, vegetable, or mineral. This attitude allows us to pollute our air, water, and food; to cause the unnecessary extinction of many species of plants and animals; and to ravage and plunder our lands, oceans, and forests. The need to dominate fellow human beings whom we fear because they are perceived as different, has spawned ethnic bigotry, sexual predation, religious exclusivism and imperialistic nationalism (tribalism) used to justify murder, rape, war, and genocide. All of these ungodly acts arise from a loss of feeling of identification with all people in the human family and the resultant fear of "the other." These are the bitter fruits when humankind and planet Earth are "sacrificed on the altar" of extreme patriarchal estrangement. This suffering has been an astronomical price to pay for the establishment of individual identity, but not one that is necessary if the illusion of separateness is tempered by the realization of connectedness.

Religion and the separation of spirit and matter

Fundamental Judeo-Christian concepts of spirit-matter dualism; religious exclusivism ("We are the chosen people of God"); polarisms of good and evil, heaven and hell; and anthropomorphic perceptions of God as an authoritarian, patriarchal Godhead (God the Father) who is separate from his creation, ruling his unquestionably obedient children from a distant throne high up in heaven, have contributed substantially to perpetuating the illusion of separateness in world consciousness. These concepts, "infused with the doctrine of original sin, the Fall of man and nature, and collective human guilt" have "severed from nature any immanent divinity" and "polarized good and evil," spirit and matter, God and man.[11] With the advent of the Protestant Reformation, these fundamental concepts became even more ensconced in human consciousness. They exposed an even more polarizing doctrine of mankind's intrinsic propensity to sin and to ultimately fall prey to the perverse instincts and natural ways of a corrupted nature due to man's "Fall" from Paradise and Original Sin. The Reformation "helped to purge the modern mind of Hellenic notions in which nature was permeated with divine rationality and final causes."[12]

The Roman Catholic Church took advantage of the perpetuating cultural illusion of separateness as it grew in moral authority and sociopolitical power in Western Europe, becoming the new

Pax Romana (Roman Empire) as Rome fell. It positioned itself in the middle of the spirit-matter polarization, between God and man, as God's sole intermediary on earth for man's redemption. Believing itself ordained by God to do so, the Church became the exclusive dispenser of God's divine truth, justice and mercy to humanity (the proverbial "middle-man"). After all, according to Christian doctrine, humankind, left to its own devices (free will, reason, intellect, rational mind, natural instincts and intuition) and a personalized connection and experience of God, would surely get lost and stray from the path of redemption into the arms of evil.

Ironically, this positioning of the Church catalyzed the reformation and, along with a millennia of restrictive ecclesiastical influences on human thought, became the wedge that further split spirit from matter, separating "deity" and "conscious design" from the dynamical functions of the cosmos and natural world. It fueled the growth of a critical scholastic secularism and naturalistic rationalism that began to spread in Western Europe at the end of the Middle Ages, hence setting the stage for the Scientific Revolution and the Age of Reason.

In an effort to safeguard the "truths" of the Christian faith, the Church either burned or concealed as heretical writings the gospels of the early Christian Gnostics that encouraged an individual experience of and relationship with God. It condemned numerous aspects of the developing trend towards rational exploration of the natural world, serving only to enlarge the growing schism between faith and reason. Thus, as Tarnas informs us, "the division between the warring adherents of reason and faith was further deepened."[13] The Church's censure of the secularist thinkers "cut off communication between the scientific thinkers and the traditional theologians, leaving the two camps increasingly aloof and distrustful toward each other."[14]

This growing tension between reason and faith was further pressured to its breaking point by the influence of the fourteenth century Franciscan monk and philosopher William of Occam and his revival of nominalism. Critical of scholasticism and the growing power of the papacy in Western Europe, Occam further severed the unity of reason and faith and cut the link between philosophy and theology. He asserted that man's mind and God's mind were not fundamentally connected and so the reason and rational thought functions of man's mind could never comprehend God and his mysteries. Such comprehension was only possible through the revelation of faith *as dictated by the Church.* Human reason, therefore, was the vehicle for revealing only the truths of the rational material world while faith was the vehicle for religious revelation of God's greater truths. Like oil and water, faith and reason could not be integrated. This belief is still fervently held by modern Christians and also underlies the doctrines of both Judaism and Islam as *fundamentally* practiced today. By this belief, Occam advocated the separation of church and state (the foundation principle upon which American democracy is founded and the U.S. Constitution was written) and opened the door for the Reformation and the Scientific Revolution, which was founded upon the mechanistic, reductionistic model of material realism. As a result, one could say Western religion was left mindless, purged of its reason and philosophical, scientific inquiry while science was left soulless, sterilized of its divine purpose and identity.

Science and the separation of mind and body

The illusion of separateness has also dominated the scientific world-view since the sixteenth century. The Scientific Revolution and the Age of Reason were born from the schism between reason and faith and the discoveries in physics, mathematics, and astronomy by such luminaries as Copernicus, Galileo, Descartes, and

Newton. These discoveries, and the reductionistic/mechanistic philosophy of science that arose concurrently, transformed the cosmos from an unfathomable figment of deific imagination into an elegant, predictable, but mindless machine, governed by precise, discernible scientific laws. This scientific model gave scholars the impression that nature could be understood completely by merely analyzing her constituent parts. It removed the concept of "conscious design," or "deity," as the source and sustainer of life and physical phenomena and relegated to the church all mystical considerations as the Church relegated all rational considerations to science. The scientific mind sterilized and dehumanized the universe by excising from it the personality and identity of Deity as *Thou,* while the religious mind purged itself of the awe and wonder of intellectual exploration into and philosophical inquiry of the mysteries of nature and God's universe (deity and the concept of conscious design in the order of the universe epitomize relationship within oneness). Science replaced *Thou* with *it* and segregated *mind* from *matter.* The mind and body were no longer viewed as one, and the self was denied recognition of its soul.

This mechanistic/reductionistic model of thought is the epistemologic foundation of *material realism* and the ideas that dominate modern conceptual models of the universe. Material realism is based on analytical and linear thinking that reduces the whole of life to the sum of its parts. It considers only the parts (the "things") that are tangible, testable and observable as real. Additionally, these parts can only be understood by reducing them to smaller parts.[15] By obsessive focus on the individual parts, this model of scientific thought often fails to encompass the integrity of the whole, the functional unity and interdependence of the parts, and the true reality of process (it prevents one from seeing the forest through the trees). It explains the existence of life as the culmination of a long series of serendipitous physio-chemical events and no more—no conscious design is intimated, suggested, or accepted. As a matter of fact, it considers the phenomenon of mind or consciousness to be only a secondary phenomenon of matter, the result of some physio-chemical conditions occurring in matter. In this conceptual model, consciousness is simply a property of the brain and life is the result of random chemical events governed by the same laws of probability as those that govern the rolling of dice.[16] In other words, life began by chance and human beings are mere clumps of protoplasm, bags of biochemical accidents walking around on two legs. This materialistic belief system leaves philosophers and other seekers of truth with an old question to ponder: "Is it in the nature of flesh to think or of bones to reason?"

Interestingly, recent research in the biochemistry of neurotransmitters has forced the scientific community to begin grudgingly reintegrating mind and body and rethinking what the human mind truly is. Neurotransmitters are the compounds (mainly amino acid derivatives) that facilitate communication between neurons in the nervous system. They are deemed the biochemical basis for thought and mood. For years, these molecules and their cell membrane receptors were assumed to be sequestered to the nervous system and unique to nervous tissue and the brain. But research by brilliant neuro-biochemists, such as Candace Pert, Ph.D., have identified cells throughout the body, in the immune system and other tissues, that synthesize, secrete, and have receptors for these same neurotransmitter compounds.[17] This startling discovery gave birth to the new discipline of psycho-neuro-immunology. It also spawned, in the minds of progressive scientists, a nagging question: If those compounds associated with thought and feeling, as well as their receptors, are found in cells all over the body, then where is the mind actually located? Where does consciousness originate?

It is prudent to refrain from judging the traditional scientific model of thought as good or bad. It simply is a model that has a definite place and purpose in the evolution of consciousness and our worldview. Mythologically, the death and dismemberment of the dragon always precedes its transformation, and the phoenix always arises from the ashes of its previous existence. Therefore, the building of a new system of scientific thought will arise from the dismembered parts of the old system.[18]

Clearly, the traditional scientific model has been responsible for a wealth of insights and discoveries into the mechanics of the physical universe. It has generated technological wonders that save lives, alleviate suffering, and greatly improve personal comfort and convenience. Nevertheless, it has reached the zenith of its conceptual validity due to its inability to adequately explain the reason and purpose for the existence of the universe, in general, and life, in particular. It fails to answer the questions "Who am I?" and "Why am I here?" Material realism has reached its limitations attempting to explain the existence of consciousness and the non-linear mathematical models needed to describe the characteristics, paradoxes, uncertainties, and probabilities of phenomena at the leading edge of human understanding (i.e., quantum physics, dissipative structures, chaos, fractals, and self-organizing systems). It has also left a deep and abiding soullessness and spiritual impoverishment at the core of our technically advanced society that has led to many ethical dilemmas and a loss of identity. By causing the indiscriminate abandoning of the spiritual heritage that provided a sense of identity, meaning, and connection to all things, our cultural story of material realism has left each of us a "me" in a world of "it" without meaningful relationship to *Thou*. It has left us wallowing in an identity crisis deplete of a deep, intimate sense of connectedness to our families, communities, ancestors, our Mother Earth and the universe that birthed us all.

But this too shall pass. This story of the "mindless machine" has served its purpose in the evolution of egoic consciousness and now, withered and faltering under the pressure of "uncertainty" and the threat of "chaos," the "probability" of its future is grim. We must surrender this story with its half-truths and illusions of separateness and fragmentation, to the contextual reality of oneness so that the *whole* of life's story can be told.

SECTION II:
Fingerprints of Identity

Chapter 4

Reawakening of the Goddess

*"There is no birth in mortal things and no end in ruinous death.
There is only mingling and interchange of parts, and this we
call nature."*

Empedocles, philosopher and scientist,
c.493–433 B.C.

*"[I] am [Protennoia, the] Thought that [dwells]
in [the Light]... [she who exists] before the All...
I am revealed in the immeasurable, ineffable (things)...
I move in every creature... I am the Invisible One within the All."*

From one of the early *Christian Nag Hammadi* texts:
Trimorphic Protennoia, XIII 35, 1–50, 24

Wholism, systems theory and the new physics

During the second half of the 20th century, the whole of
life's story has been culturally re-emerging from the
decaying matter of dogmatic beliefs and the mechanistic
narrative in the guise of the "new physics," systems theory, the science of chaos, studies in consciousness, environmental/ecological
awareness, and the "wholistic" movement. This re-emerging story
is the "old story" of nature that has always been told by every seed,

plant, river and stone; the one our civilization has stopped listening to. It addresses the developing unitive conception of the cosmos and its underlying conscious design. It is rejoining reason and faith, spirit and matter as it draws upon spiritual traditions that have survived the weathering of centuries of restrictive, exclusive dogma, and integrates them into contemporary quantum theory to answer both old and new questions about the nature of consciousness, matter, and the universe from a more comprehensive perspective. As a matter of fact, one marvels at how much contemporary scientists are beginning to sound like ancient mystics as they are coming to the old realization that fragmentation is an illusion and wholeness is the reality.[1] In the words of theoretical physicist David Bohm, "Wholeness is what is real and fragmentation is the response of this whole to man's action, guided by illusory perception, which is shaped by fragmentary thought."[2]

This re-emerging old story has also begun to influence the medical sciences re-establishing awareness of the "mind-body" connection and the essential union of human life with all other living things. This reawakening has led to a great resurgence of interest in the more traditional and "natural" healing practices, (e.g., Ayurvedic and traditional Chinese medicine, naturopathic medicine and homeopathy) which have always maintained a "wholistic" or contextual view of the patient and the healing process.

In biology and the life sciences, the old story is now being told anew by "Systems Theory." The integration of systems thinking into scientific thought has also shifted scholarly attention from parts to the whole, from objects to relationships. Formulated in the early twentieth century by organismic biologists, Gestalt psychologists, and ecologists, systems theory has been gradually incorporated into the scientific mainstream over the past sixty to seventy years. Recent discoveries in quantum physics, nonlinear mathematics, and chaos theory have further accelerated its integration into the latest scientific models of the cosmos.[3]

Systems theory has begun to dramatically influence the environmental and atmospheric sciences, evolutionary biology and genetics, and other scientific disciplines. It has been used as the nucleus for new conceptual models to explain the origins and development of living systems and is answering some of the long-standing, perplexing questions in these fields. The "rediscovery" of systems modeling may be viewed by future historians as the turning point away from the limited mechanistic story of fragmentation toward the old story of nature and wholeness.

Physicist Fritjof Capra summarizes the key characteristics of systems thinking quite clearly in his book, *The Web of Life*, when he writes:

> The first, and most general, criterion [for systems thinking] is the shift from the parts to the whole. Living systems are integrated wholes whose properties can not be reduced to those of smaller parts. Their essential, or 'systemic,' properties are properties of the whole, which none of the parts have. They arise from the 'organizing relations' of the parts—that is, from a configuration of ordered relationships...[4]

In the systems view, the objects themselves are networks of relationships, embedded in larger networks. "For the systems thinker, the relationships are primary."[5] It is our opinion that this focus on the relationships, and the whole instead of the parts, is a manifestation of the Thou reawakening in human consciousness, allowing again the fusion of spirit and matter.

Iteration, feedback loops and non-linearity

The genesis of "systems thinking" is rooted in the growing knowledge of non-linearity, communication networks, iteration, and feedback loops. Such phenomena permit the characteristic self-regulation and self-organization fundamental to all living systems. To describe appropriately the mechanisms of iteration and feedback loops that underlie the phenomena of self-regulation and self-organization, scientists have had to delve into the chaotic world of non-linear mathematical equations.

Non-linear mathematics has become an integral part of systems thinking because, as John Briggs and David Peat point out, "The non-linear world is wholistic: it's a world where everything is interconnected, so there must always be a subtle order present."[6] It appears as though the language of life's story is non-linear, and the only way to understand its mystery is through non-linear equations (i.e., equations forming a parabola as opposed to a straight line on a Cartesian grid $y = x^2$ as opposed to $y = x + 1$.

In non-linear mathematics, very small changes in one variable can have enormous impact on other variables through repeated iteration. By duplicating over and over life's fundamental process of self-reflection, non-linear equations have provided great insight into the *real world* of natural living systems, which commonly function in a non-linear, non-mechanical, chaotic fashion.[7] In nature, simple, easily-analyzed, mechanistic linear systems appear to be an aberration from the norm: chaos, uncertainty, non-linearity and continuous change rule.

In the natural world, iteration generates self-regulating information feedback loops that establish dynamic balance among all elements of a living system. This is known as homeostasis. This dynamic balance allows a system to self-organize. Additionally, feedback loops produce *dramatic outcomes from small changes* within a system.[8] Because of this activity, tiny, barely perceptible influences in some minute aspect of a system can, over time, produce profound outcomes for the whole of that system. In such cases, exact predictions of outcomes from minute influences, especially in terms of quantifiable absolutes, are impossible. The language of probability is more accurately descriptive and enlightening in this realm. Welcome to the torturous insecurity of uncertainties in the real, living world!

The development of and integration into the sciences of a systems-based, wholistic model is inducing a resurrection of the Thou of "Deity" and the idea of "conscious design" in the fabric of the living universe. It is also stimulating a growing re-realization of the interconnectedness and interdependence we humans have with all living things on this planet. It is forcing us to conceptually reassemble the dismantled parts of the supposedly soulless machine, with a deeper appreciation of the actual nature and function of the parts, based on their contextual relationship to the whole.

We are rediscovering that the whole—the machine—is not mindless after all! She is alive, organic, conscious and self-aware! She is the Goddess, the physical embodiment of spirit.

> She is the personification of the primal element named in the second verse of Genesis, where we read that "the spirit of God moved upon *the face of the waters.*" In the Hindu myth, she is the female figure through whom the Self begot all creatures. More abstractly understood, she is the world-bounding frame: "space, time, and causality"—the shell of the cosmic egg. More abstractly still, she is the lure that moved the Self-brooding Absolute to the act of creation.[9]

Individuality and the ambiguity of part and whole

Earlier in Chapter Two, we discussed the conundrum that arises when one ponders the ambiguity of "part" and "whole." Is the part an individual, or is the whole the individual? If each is dependent upon the other, where does the individual, "the self" begin and where does it end? Is a part just some incomplete fragment of the whole or is it a whole unto itself, with its own individual parts? Just what defines a part as a part or a whole as a whole? To gain insight into this puzzle, we turn to science writer and philosopher Arthur Koestler, who wrote:

> A "part," as we generally use the word, means something fragmentary and incomplete, which by itself would have no legitimate existence. On the other hand, a "whole" is considered as something complete in itself, which needs no further explanation. But "wholes" and "parts" in this absolute sense just do not exist anywhere, either in the domain of living organisms or of social organizations. What we find are intermediary structures on a series of levels in an ascending order of complexity: sub-wholes which display, according to the way you look at them, some of the characteristics commonly attributed to wholes and some of the characteristics commonly attributed to parts.[10]

Koestler has named these sub-wholes "holons," because they behave "partly as wholes or wholly as parts." These holons, he explains, are "possessed of two opposite tendencies or potentials: an integrative tendency to function as a part of the larger whole, and a self-assertive tendency to preserve its individual autonomy."[11] Egoic consciousness, as a representative of the self-assertive tendency, commonly favors viewing its "self" as a whole in a world of subordinate parts. We propose that every individual, every existing thing is a holon: a "self" that functions as a "part" for a larger whole, as well as being a whole made up of individual parts. Every individual is caught in this paradoxical tension of part and whole just as is the "Great Whole" itself. This is the tension of being that forms and shapes ego consciousness and self-identity. Due to this paradox, Koestler likens each individual or holon to the Roman god Janus, who has two faces looking in opposite directions *(Fig. 4-1).* As with Janus, every individual has one face that looks infinitely inward toward the subordinate levels from the vantage point of a self-contained whole, and another face that looks infinitely outward at the greater whole from the vantage of a dependent part.

> From organelles to organs, from organisms living in symbiosis to societies with more complex forms of interdependence, we nowhere find completely self-contained wholes, only holons—double-faced entities which display the characteristics both of independent units and of inter-dependent parts.[12]

Fig. 4-1. Janus, the double-faced god.

It has become clear that no single property of a part can be fully understood without understanding its contextual relationship to the whole.[13] Therefore, to understand life's story and to answer the question, "Who am I?" and to live your true self-affirmation, you must first understand the network of relationships that comprise the Great Whole of everything that is, of which you are a part, your place within that whole and the whole's identity and nature. You must then live consciously and contextually your true identity *as both part and whole* concurrently.

Yet for the curious mind, deeper questions abound. "What is the nature and essence of this Great and Boundless Whole?" Is it all of life, the whole universe, God? Is it a holon as well, endlessly in relationship with itself? What is my relationship to this whole? How can I better realize who I am as my "self" and as the whole? Would a better understanding of the whole provide a better understanding of myself and visa versa? It is our view that meaningful answers to these questions can arise spontaneously when the whole of life's story is revealed. In the following chapters we will attempt to do this by presenting what we feel to be the identifiable fundamental principles that generate and govern the nature and activity of living systems as described by biologists, psychologists, physicists, philosophers and mystics. We believe these principles are rooted in the quest of consciousness for identity and self-awareness, for meaning. We suggest all forms of living systems are dynamic constructs of recursive, iterative, integrated patterns (networks of relationships) that defy entropy as they evolve through chaos on the path of continuous creation. These patterns are based on the primary theme of self-reflection through relationship. Through self-reflection in the "mirror" of relationship, consciousness, as life, discovers its "self," becomes self-aware and self-conscious, thereby realizing its identity—its meaning. In the words of the Kabbalists, "Only through relationship can God know God" and only through the mirror of creation can "The Face gaze upon The Face."

We suggest the quest for identity and meaning is the driving force that propels life away from the entropic death of non-being through the transformational death of chaos into the resurrection of new order and evolvement upon its path of continuous creation. This quest for identity also propels consciousness into the illusion of fragmentation where the egoic *I* of separateness is ultimately sacrificed upon the altar of relationship in the fire of chaos for the *Thou* of wholeness and contextuality to be realized. All healing is a function of this process of self-discovery and transformation into wholeness while all disease is the chaotic, transformational element integral to that process. Health is not health without the ever-present possibility and existential reality of disease. Therefore, disease is not a thing to be eliminated, "cut out" or suppressed. It is instead, a *dynamic process of life* through which one must pass, through which one is transformed. It all starts with The Beginning.

*"Oh, grant me my prayer, that I may never
lose the touch of The One in the play of The Many."*

Rabindranath Tagore, Indian poet
1861–1941

Chapter 5

The Mirror and the Universe—
Reflecting on God

"In an instant, rise from time and space.
Set the world aside and become a world within yourself."

Shabestari, Persian Sufi and poet,
c. 1250–1320

Symmetries of life and the adventure of becoming

There is symmetry in nature and the universe. It is the symmetry of *self-similarity across scale*. It implies recursion (pattern inside of pattern); repetition of a theme infinitely projected through all levels of scale from the macrocosmic down to the microcosmic and visa versa.[1] This symmetry exists because of fundamental laws that govern and direct equally in every location in space and moment in time the creative unfolding of *The One* as *The One* affirms its being as life. In the early civilizations of Egypt and Persia, this symmetry was recognized as a universal law and was stated in the Emerald Tablets of Hermes: "As above, so below; as in heaven, so also on earth." In other words, as *The One* becomes *The Many*, Its nature and essence as the whole are expressed and reiterated in *The Many* as its parts. As all the characters in life's continuous story, *The Many* are made in the image and likeness of *The One*—their Source and Creator—because they are *The One*.

As *The Many* evolve through the circular, self-reflective, recursive movement of the cycle of life (the "cosmogonic cycle"), the fundamental laws of creation constantly guide and direct their evolvement. Thus *The Many*, as the parts, elaborate the essence and nature of the whole in their every form, shape, activity, conscious act and unconscious motivation over the immense range of their diversity. There is one caveat, however. Though *The Many* evolve via the symmetry of self-similarity guided by the fundamental laws of creation, their individual, evolutionary paths are not predetermined because of "free will" and its associated act of "free choice," as discussed in Chapter Two.

Because of choice and free will, the unfolding of *The One* into *The Many* proceeds creatively, under the influence of Heisenberg's uncertainty principle, along novel paths not fated or predestined by *The One*. The unfolding is only probabilistic—a kind of "probabilistic determinism." Any suggestion or appearance of predetermination is due to the recurrent patterns and symmetries in the unfolding process and the probability of specific outcomes dictated by the pattern of choices made by *The Many*. These patterns and symmetries are the "fingerprints" or "hallmarks" of *The One's* essential nature (the personality of deity) reflected in *The One's* characteristic expression of Itself as *The Many*. In a sense, because of free will, the many characters in life's continuing story have been engaged, empowered, and encouraged by *The One* to be conscious participants in their own creation (i.e., *co-creators*). *The One* created the universe, and *The Many*, as *The One*, create everything else. This is reflected in Genesis 1:26, "And God said, Let *us* make man in our image, after our likeness," as the Hebraic pleural form (Elohim) of the name of God is used.[2]

Within the symmetries and influence of the natural laws of the universe, there seems to be ample room in the evolution of life for asymmetry and symmetry-breaking experimentation leading to the development of novelty and diversity. As a matter of fact, such experimentation appears to be the rule and may well be a key characteristic of *The One's* true nature. The evolutionary process has clearly demonstrated an impulsive-like, exploratory and experimental quality. Throughout life's evolving story on this planet, there have been many trials and errors and many successes. Numerous species and traits have come and gone while many have persisted as *The One* explores Its capacity for creativity within the bounds of its nature and essence. Like any good story, some characters are killed off while others persist to develop in complexity. As every good scientist and storyteller knows, the best one can ever hope for within the most fundamental laws of the universal story are "probabilities" due to life's "uncertainties."

Free will is the symmetry-breaking catalyst that generates the uncertainties in life's evolvement. It is *The One's* "prime directive" that is written into every line of life's evolving story. It contributes greatly to the experimental nature of the evolutionary process and allows for the immense diversity and variety expressed by biological systems. The probabilities and uncertainties it generates keep life exciting and adventurous. Without free will there would be no self-discovery, no answering of the primal question, "Who or what am I?"

We suggest the emergence of every new life form, from the time of the very beginning (if a beginning even exists) to the present, has been simply *The One* discovering a new aspect of *The One's* being from a simple single-cell organism to human life. The essential self-sustaining processes of life (self-regulation, self-organization, reproduction, growth, adaptation and evolution) are processes of *The One* discovering itself as it affirms itself in all of its possible manifestations and combinations. In this context, we believe life is the dynamic process of reply to the question of identity. It is *The One's* own hero journey and discovery quest. It is the result of the "essential self-affirmation" of *The One* expressing and discovering the true essence and nature of its being as it creatively and continuously unfolds into *The Many* for the purpose of entering into relationship with itself so that it may know itself by experiencing itself. According to Kabbalistic tradition, the Hebraic names of God assigned to the first three emanations of God's being, represented as the first three Sephirot of the Kabalistic Tree of Life *(Fig. 5-1)*, are EHYEH, YAHVEH and ELOHIM respectively. These names of God, literally translate into: "I AM—to become—God as *The Many*."[3]

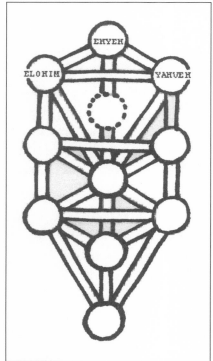

Fig. 5-1. The Kabalistic Tree of Life *with its ten Sefirot (spheres or vessels) representing the ten Attributes of God from which the universe was created. The structure of the* Tree of Life *is formed by the relationship of the sefirot to each other, which is determined by the 22 Paths of Illumination connecting them.*

Before the beginning

There appears to be a point of agreement between the many creation myths of the world and modern science concerning the beginning of the universe. They agree there was chaos—the world was "without form and void"—before the beginning, and out of this chaos order emerged in the form of the Universe. However, no one really knows for sure what was before the beginning. More so, no one truly understands yet what the beginning was, if it was at all! There are only theories and speculations based on existing tell-tale evidence revealed in astrophysics through the movement of galaxies and in quantum physics through the birth and death of elemental particles and their interactions with the four forces (electromagnetism, gravity, and the strong and weak nuclear forces). From a physics perspective, the infinitely high temperatures attained just prior to the Big Bang present a major problem for understanding what occurred before the beginning. They erased all evidence of what may have been before.[4] Hence, we are left to speculation and theory.

There is another point of agreement between the theological, mythological and mystical communities that seems to be consistent with the latest scientific theory: Out of the chaos of nothingness came a period of "Grand Unification" just prior to the creation of the universe. The scientific community informs us that all matter and the forces acting upon it were unified into One Absolute All, a Singularity just prior to the "Big Bang."[5] There is one bit of information, however, the scientific community has so far failed to provide: the reason for the beginning.

As stated earlier, many systems of Western theology, philosophy, and mysticism, suggest the issue of identity, God's desire to know what God is, originally catalyzed the birth of the universe. This is the fundamental theme of creation in the Jewish Kabbalistic system, the root of Christian and Jewish mystical traditions.[6] As Kabbalist and author Rabbi Z'ev ben Shimon Halevi writes, "Tradition states that God willed to see God." God, therefore, created "so as to make a place wherein the mirror of Existence might manifest" so that "God might behold God."[7] This phenomenon of God gazing upon God is also alluded to in the ancient *Egyptian Book of the Dead,* where it reads:

> I am the divine hidden Soul who creates the gods, and who gives sepulchral meals to the denizens of the underworld, of the deep, and of heaven. I am the rudder of the east, the possessor of two divine faces wherein His beams are seen.[8]

It is fascinating how much this "mystical tradition" of God beholding God seems to parallel the observation phenomenon described in quantum physics. The observer of an event is never objectively removed or separate from that event but is an active participant in it and, as such, effects the outcome of that event.[9] It appears as though the observer, through the act of observing, gives an event meaning, thereby making it real.[10]

As God beholds God or consciousness enters into the illusion of separateness and observes its *self* (compares and contrasts its *self* with the outside world of *non-self*), it becomes real to itself by becoming self-aware. Through that self-awareness, it defines and continually redefines itself in each successive moment of observation *ad infinitum*. Observation is the continuing phenomenon of consciousness that produces the internal, subjective experience of "selfness" or "*I*-ness." With ongoing observation, the realization of self by consciousness expands.

At this point, one begins to wonder: If the universe exists because "God wished to see God," then who or what is this "God" of pre-creation existence who wished to see itself? In numerous theological and mystical traditions this God of pre-creation existence is known as "the self-existent infinite Being, without likeness or reflection."[11] It was, and is, existence beyond existence, in which, according to the Hindu Rig-Veda, "neither non-being nor being was as yet" because there was no separation, nothing else outside that existence to compare, contrast, and thus define that existence.[12] God was, but at the same time, God was not because God had yet to be defined into being by a reflective counterpart through the illusion of maximal contrast. (When *only one thing* exists and *nothing else,* that one thing isn't anything because there is nothing else to compare and contrast that one thing against to give it definition—not even a nothing.) There was only the unmanifest allness of chaos: "The Absolute," the "Transcendent All that is Nothing," "Beingness without Being," the "Supreme Ultimate," the "Rootless Root," the unfathomable and unknowable "Causeless Cause," and so on. According to the Tao Te Ching, this precreation state "can not be grasped" because it "is forever undefined."[13] It is *The One* as the "Unmanifest Creator," before the creation. It was all and yet it was nothing because it was not yet realized into something. Kabbalistically, it was the state before the beginning in which God did not gaze upon God because "The Face of God" did not yet exist to be gazed upon.[14]

Before the beginning, there was no time or spatial orientation. There was only the endless potential of chaos in "the undefined, endless now and forever" of eternal being before the coming of the opposites and the birth of *The Many.* This state is depicted in Taoist philosophy as the *Wu Chi*—the empty circle. Because of the symmetries of life, this state of existence (before the beginning) is recapitulated through all life forms as the prenatal time in the womb of the mother. It is also, as Neumann points out, "the time of existence in paradise where the psyche has her pre-worldly abode, the time before the birth of the ego, the time of unconscious envelopment, of swimming in the ocean of the unborn."[15] By mythological and mystical tradition, this was the epoch of the unconscious, *non*-self-aware consciousness (the time in Paradise) during which the self-conscious potential had not yet become condensed and ordered into the singularity of self.

The finitude of the human mind prevents us from ever even beginning to accurately conceive of such an abstract absolute state. It is an unimaginable enigma that no mind can ever fathom and no language can ever describe. Nevertheless, in the following pages we will attempt, in spite of our feeble tools and limiting language, to describe the processes by which we believe God, as *The One*, brought about the creation of *The Many*. Our intention in presenting this information is to provide the reader with a plausible outline of life's continuing story as we have begun to understand it. This is done in hopes the reader might gain a deeper insight into the nature and identity of *The One* and, by so doing, gain a deeper insight into the nature and identity of his/her self.

The first separation

From the conscious potential of the "endless now and forever" before the beginning of time and space, *The One* that was *All*, willed the first separation so that *The One* might behold itself in the face of *The Many*. And out of the chaos of non-being came the order of being.[16] This first separation set the stage for the illusion of maximal contrast and polarity enabling the eventual development of self-aware consciousness (See Chapter Two). According to many creation myths, this first separation occurred as the separation of "the World Parents" or the separation of the earth from the sky. Often these symbolic dyads are identical. Commonly, the mother parent is associated with the earth (the germinating, nurturing womb of all substance and matter, representing the symmetry of the container) while the father parent is associated with the sky or the sun (the force that acts upon the earth, representing the asymmetry of dynamic process impregnating the womb of matter).[17] In Genesis 1:1, this idea is expressed as God

creating the heaven and the earth.[18] However, in more mystical traditions, the first separation is depicted as a phenomenon
accomplished by "a contraction in the Absolute All, so as to make
a place wherein the mirror of existence might manifest."[19]

The gravitational force of love

In astrophysics, gravity is the force that holds heavenly bodies
in dynamic relationships we call star systems and galaxies. In particle physics, the strong nuclear force keeps the fundamental
particles of matter tightly held together to form the nucleus of an
atom. These two forces may be two different aspects of the same
force (i.e., the greater unifying force called love). In a fashion analogous to gravity and the strong nuclear force, love draws *all
individual parts of the whole into relationship and holds them there.*
Love is the attractive force that draws and holds each one of us
into relationships of meaning and significance. Stimulated by the
provocative nature of will, the gravitational force of love, as the
"Spirit of God," "moved upon the face of the waters" and caused
the first contraction or in-breathing of "The Absolute All."[20]

The gravitational action of love was initiated by will. The will
of God to see God lured the Self-brooding Absolute to the act of
creation. It caused love to draw the self-conscious potential of
The Absolute All together into the "Divine Singularity" of *The
One* of God.

For the sake of example only, this contraction may be visualized
or imagined as a spiraling vortex (like a whirlpool, tornado or spiraling galaxy) drawing all peripheral trajectories internally to a
central point *(Fig. 5-2)*. Scientists and mathematicians can perhaps
envision this phenomenon as a kind of Belousov-Zhabotinsky reaction.*(Fig. 5-3)* This is a well-known reaction in which initially
random and chaotic motions of molecules in a solution spontaneously self-organize and give rise to spiraling, circulating
structures in space and time.[21] Thus can order arise from chaos.

Fig. 5-2.

Fig. 5-3. The Belousov-Zhabotinsky reaction is an example of the spiraling, iterative structures that can spontaneously occur (autocatalyze) in a fluid medium when the right temperature and the right mixture of chemicals are present. These structures can self-reproduce and generate various levels of complexity. They are microscosmic representations of the macrocosmic event of creation.

This original, spiraling organizational pattern was to become the womb of potential wherein the seed of self-consciousness and Manifest Existence would arise.*(Fig. 5-4a,b)* The space in which this act of creation took place can be considered as something analogous to the abstract mathematical construct known as "phase space." Phase space is a kind of "cyberspace" or "virtual reality space" into which complex dynamic mathematical relationships and equations can be projected. In truth, however, this initial creative act did not occupy time or space because it was pre-temporal and pre-spatial.

Fig. 5-4a.
Celtic stone carving from the Newgrange burial chamber in County Meath, Ireland, c. 3000 B.C.

Fig. 5-4b. Celtic spiral design carved in stone slab at Alberlemno, Angus, Scotland. Notice how much these Celtic spirals resemble the Belosov-Zhabatinsky reaction.

Numerous designs like these are found throughout the ancient Celtic world. Are they representations of the primal dynamical process from which the universe was created?

Some creation myths have called this womb of potential "The Void." But it was not, however, a true void.[22] It was *filled with the potential of all that was to come.* It was like an idea of a story in the author's mind before that story is written.

Out of the void

The study of the void as a physical vacuum suggests the primal *womb of potential,* although pre-temporal and pre-spatial, was not completely empty. It had to contain, within its faculties, *the potential of everything* that the laws of nature would allow.[23] As physicist Henning Genz informs us, "The physical vacuum, which in the course of history has made its appearance in human thought under as varying a set of names as nothing, the void, space, materia prima (Aristotle), matter (Plotinus), and the ether, carries within itself the possibilities of everything that can exist in the physical world."[24] The primal womb was most likely filled with a patterned, consciousness potential *(Fig. 5-5)*; something likened to what we can best describe in the terminology of modern physics as a "field potential" at absolute zero temperature and "zero-point energy." Excited by the triggering energy impulse of the Will of God to see God, this patterned, consciousness potential self-organized, determining through its own characteristic patterns of fundamental dynamic processes, what virtual particles would be generated and what properties and probabilities would manifest.[25]

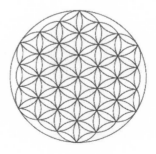

Fig. 5-5. A limited conception of what the primal quantum or spatial field pattern might look like based on an iteration of the vesica pisces and the three fundamental creative archetypes represented by the point, line and circle.

All that comprises the physical universe, all matter and the forces that affect it, are now believed by physicists to be manifestations of some form of a quantum field. In reality, there appears to be nothing else in the Universe except fields. In the words of Cambridge University astrophysicist John Gribbin, "The Universe can be thought of as made up of a variety of interacting fields alone, with the particles representing the quanta of each field, manifested in obedience to the rules of wave-particle duality and the uncertainty principle."[26]

Conception

As taught in mystical traditions, a *dimensionless point* or singularity formed at the center of the Void as the contraction occurred. It may have been similar to an "attractor point" in mathematics, which is a point in "phase space" that, like the center of a whirlwind or a whirlpool, exerts a powerful attraction, pulling towards itself all peripheral trajectories.[27] In the Kabalistic tradition, this singularity is symbolized by *aleph*, the first letter of the Hebrew alphabet. It is emblematic of the "first cause," the "Divine singularity" or "Divine seed." It is the nucleus of dynamic process within the mythological "cosmic egg" from which the universe would arise. As with the nucleus of any egg or cell, the singularity had to carry within it all the pattern information and potential needed for the development of self-aware consciousness so that such consciousness could recognize and affirm its own identity. This was the "pregnant point" referred to in the "Hindu Hymn of Creation" in the *Rig-Veda*.[28] Within it lay the concentrated, indrawn potential and identity pattern of The Absolute All from which all matter, form and individuated consciousness would arise. It was the exterior of Absolute All now drawn into the interior through the spiraling motion of the vortex so that an internal, subjective experience of self could be had. It is analogous to DNA, the biological "Ark of the Covenant" within the nucleus of every cell through which *The One* becomes *The Many* and directs the unfolding of particular aspects of its nature.

Now, in the original creative process, there were two: the point and the circle, the inside and the outside. The point, as the seed of dynamic process, was contained in the circle of the womb (as the vessel contains the seed and the exterior contains the interior). The point represents *I,* while the circle represents *Thou.* The "Divine Seed" of all existence was suspended in the unconscious envelopment of the primal womb of chaos "that was without form and void." The original seed pattern of consciousness from which the world was to arise was "swimming in the ocean of the unborn" and then "the Spirit of God moved upon the face of the waters."[29]

It is taught in Kabalistic tradition that the Will of God penetrated the void of the Cosmic Egg and "moved upon the face of its waters" as the single sperm penetrates the ovum (egg) for conception.[30] *(Fig. 5-6)* In this context, we suggest that Deific Will expressed itself as an energy fluctuation in the "field potential" of the primal womb of chaos to ignite the first contraction and impregnate the seed nucleus with the identity pattern of all that was to come. It did this by imprinting the "face of the waters" (its "field potential") with the organizational pattern or "spatial field pattern" *(Fig. 5-5)* of the self-aware consciousness of manifest existence. We believe this action concurrently initiated the most essential dynamic process of self-reflection and circular recursion known to science, defining the primary distinctions between inside and outside, self and non-self. According to mathematician Stan Tenen, founder of the Meru Foundation, the 3, 10 torus knot projected onto a dimpled sphere torus best illustrates this dynamic process.*(Figs. 5-7 & 5-8)* Its central vortex is the singular point.

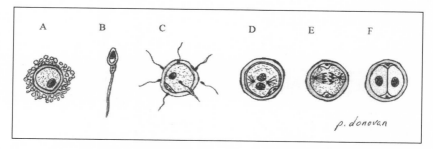

Fig. 5-6. Fertilization of the Primary Oocyte and First Division of the Fertilized Egg

A. *Female egg or primary oocyte representing the cosmic egg or vessel of creation.*
B. *Male sperm representing the will of God.*
C. *Spermatozoon penetrating the oocyte initiating fertilization. (This act reiterates the will of God penetrating the void of the cosmic egg, "and the spirit of God moved upon the face of its waters.")*
D. *Male and female pronuclei of the fertilized oocyte. (The chromosomes are ready to be combined and paired in the nucleus of the cell to become the biological "Ark of the Covenant.")*
E. *Chromosomes moving to opposite poles for cell division to take place so that the monad may become the diad. (This act reiterates the "first separation" of the mythological world parents of heaven and earth.)*
F. *Two-cell stage of early development. (From the diad, the many are born as each cell continues the process of division and differentiation until a whole organism is created.)*

Fig. 5-7. Standard ring form of the 3, 10 Torus Knot. This is the standard ring form of one continuous filament forming three rings and ten loops/knots.

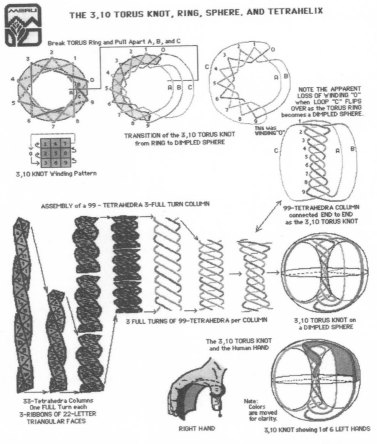

K,R,S,T.jpg 2feb7 @'92,'97 S. Tenen / MERU Fdtn, POB 503, Sharon, MA 02067 (781) 784-8902 meru1@well.com http://www.meru.org

Fig. 5-8. The 3, 10 Torus Knot, Ring, Sphere, and Tetrahelix by Stan Tenen. Used with permission. Fig. 5-8. shows:

- *How the standard "Ring" form of the 3,10 trus knot can be transformed to fit on the surface of a dimpled-sphere torus.*
- *Hos the 3,10 torus knot is defined by a "touch-pad magic squre" whose diagonals, central row, and column add to 15.*
- *How a specially-shaped dimpled sphere form of the 3, 10 torus knot can define 6 hand-shaped regions wound around a (6-thumb) tetrahelical central column.*
- *How the central column of the dimpled-sphere form of the 3, 10 torus knot is complosed of and defined by a column of 99-tetrahedra.*
- *How each hand is defined by a central column (wound on the thumb and extended over the palm and 4 fingers) of a "jubilee" of 49-tetrahedra; and*
- *How the 99-tetrahedron tetrahedral column consists of 3 ribbons of 3 x 22 = 66 trangular faces, with one triangular face for each of the 22 letters of 3 strings of 3 Hebrew alphabets.*

Outside-in, inside-out

The dimpled sphere torus is basically a 2-torus, (i.e., a spinning doughnut shaped vortex like a smoke ring).*(Fig.5-9)* The 2-torus is unique among all solid geometric forms because it can continually fold in on itself, reflecting itself to itself as it turns on a central axis. This movement represents "The Face" gazing upon "The Face" or God beholding God. Through this dynamic motion,

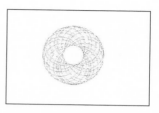

Fig. 5-9. The 2-torus. The most basic vortextual shape. It spins circularly as it also rotates in on itself. Courtesy of Julian Sprott, Ph.D.

self-reflection and continuous creation are assured—the seed, produces the tree, that makes the fruit, that carries the seed that produces the tree, and so on. As Tenen states, "It represents the reflexive, self-organizing process that is the natural transformation and unfoldment of every 'seed' (Singularity) via its 'tree' (Unfoldment) into new 'fruit' (Wholeness) of its kind."[31]

The spiraling vortex of the 3, 10 torus knot is based upon the unitary reciprocal or hyperbolic spiral. This spiral mathematically and geometrically illustrates *The One* unfolding into *The Many* in continuous creation. It demonstrates the transition from inside to outside and outside to inside as it reaches between an inner point and an outer expanse through the continuing transformation of circular-spiraling and linear extension and contraction. As this spiral (the pattern of consciousness) is projected onto a cube-octahedral sphere (the womb of The Absolute All), the infinite end of the spiraling curve becomes finite in space but infinite in process. It is infinite in process because it continually turns back on itself, repeating the process in a manner that forms the central spiraling filament of the 3, 10 torus knot and the dimpled spheroid of this geometric structure. This pattern, as theorized by Tenen, may be emblematic of the dynamic process for all life.[32]

We believe this act of creation began the recurring thematic phenomena (enfolding and unfolding, inspiration and expiration, receiving and giving) which establish the basic rhythms of life that beat every heart, inspire every breath, and birth every seed. As the outside is enfolded inside, the interior qualifies the exterior through contrast and comparison, thereby giving it identity and meaning. But by doing so, it also qualifies itself, giving itself an internalized, subjective experience of identity and meaning. This act may reflect the very nature of consciousness, (i.e., to *give identity and meaning to itself and the outside world*).

Consciousness takes in the external world and qualifies it into an internalized, subjective experience, giving both the experience and itself identity and meaning.

The purpose of consciousness is to give identity and meaning to itself and the outside world.

Consciousness takes in the outside world of *Thou*, and then molds and qualifies it into the internal experience of *I*. In other words; consciousness takes in the outer, non-local world of unmanifest quantum potential and collapses it into the local material reality of particle manifestation. By so doing, consciousness "chooses" its reality and, by that choice, *chooses its identity*. We see this process in action in Genesis 2:19 as follows: "And out of the ground the Lord God formed every beast of the field, and every fowl of the air; and brought them unto Adam to see what he would call them: and whatsoever Adam called every living creature, that was the name thereof."[33]

Here the Biblical first man (the archetype of self-aware, egoic consciousness), incorporating into his interior consciousness his sensations and experiences of his external surroundings, qualifies them by giving them identity. He, in-turn, is transformed by this experience and is himself given identity through his relationship to the external world established by his experience of it. This process forms the bedrock upon which egoic consciousness and personality are structured.

As this internalization of the exterior proceeds, the interior unfolds the ever-evolving new identity back to the exterior like the blossoming of a flower, and the cycle continues *ad infinitum.* This process is ubiquitous in living systems and may be used to define life. In living organisms, the outer world is taken in (ingested, inspired, absorbed, impregnated), processed (digested, metabolized, nurtured) and modified (assimilated, developed) to reaffirm life and self-identity through continuous creation. That which is taken in is transformed in some way and then given back (excreted, secreted, expired, birthed), only to be taken in again at another time, in another form. In the whole of this recursive cycle of life nothing is ever lost. All energy and matter, every *I* and *Thou,* is recycled to be born again, used again, transformed again, and affirmed again endlessly in more novel and ever-increasingly complex and magnificent forms.

The "Three Hidden Splendors"

Through the "Three Hidden Splendors" of Creative Intelligence, the Will of God fertilized the Cosmic Egg of God's own potential (the Void), and the cosmogonic cycle of life began. The Three Hidden Splendors are primary attributes of Deity symbolized geometrically by the *point, circle,* and *line.* The *point* represents "the pregnant point" of the Divine Singularity. The *circle* represents the periphery of the Cosmic Egg—the container. The *line* (the radius between the point and the circle) represents Divine Will and acts as a vector defining the direction for the unfolding process of creation. As all geometric forms are generated from the *point, line* and *circle*, all life comes forth from these three basic elements of creative intelligence. At the moment of the first separation and contraction, the Three Hidden Splendors of Creative Intelligence were awakened in the light of self-consciousness and set forth to direct the unfolding of *The One* into *The Many*. These three essential creative attributes of *The One* can be seen as constituents of a distinctive signature, fingerprint, or hallmark of *The One's* nature and personality, and can be defined as:

Mind:

The influence that designs the pattern of organization, defining the form and structure of that which is created. It "informs matter" of the relationships of the fundamental particles of matter. The pattern may be likened to what is known in physics as a spatial field or quantum field.

Substance:

The material that manifests the design by conforming to the pattern in order to bring the concept of the conscious design into fruition. The conforming constituents of substance are the fundamental particles of matter that enter into the complex, dynamic relationships as atomic and molecular configurations, regulated by the field-defined laws of physics and chemistry.

Power:

The energy that catalyzes and fuels the processes of creation and maintains the structure and form of substance in accordance with the pattern of conscious design. It may be perceived as energy and the four fundamental forces in nature (gravity, the strong and weak nuclear forces, and electromagnetism).

We will discuss these principles in greater detail in the following chapter.

And "The Word" was made manifest

The Light of Will, the Will of God to see God, was projected to the "Divine Singularity" and the original conception of "I AM" took place. At that moment, the light of conscious self-realization was ignited, "And God saw the light," and realized "that it was good."[34] The Will of Divine Self-Affirmation had fertilized the Cosmic Egg of potential self-aware consciousness and caused the Manifest Universe to come into being through the light of self-realization. As the Zohar proclaims: "The divine germ from which emanated and expanded the boundless ether appeared, and this ether became differentiated into form and color giving rise to the universe...."[35] "Then God knew (as the *Hindu Brihadaranyaka Upanishad* proclaims): 'Indeed I am myself the creation, for I have projected the entire world.' Whence he was called Creation...."[36] Heated to an infinitely high temperature by the burning desire to affirm Deific identity into manifestation and behold its splendor, the will of God to see God brought forth this moment of the beginning. In more scientific terms, this could be likened to the moment of the Big Bang when, according to physicist Brian Greene, "the whole universe erupted from a microscopic nugget whose size makes a grain of sand look colossal."[37]

Time had begun. Its great pendulum, whose beats are the ages, commenced to vibrate. The era of creation or manifestation had at last arrived. The *nekuda reshima,* primal point or nucleus, appeared. From it emanated and expanded the primary substance, the illimitable phosphorescent ether, of the nature of light, formless, colorless, being neither black nor green nor red. In it, latent yet potentially as in a mighty womb, lay the myriad of prototypes and

numberless forms of all created things as yet indis-
cernible indistinguishable. By the secret and silent
action of the divine will, from this primal luminous
point, radiated forth the vital life-giving spark which,
pervading and operating in the great etheric ocean of
forms, became the soul of the universe, the fount
and origin of all mundane life and motion and terres-
trial existence, and in its nature and essence and
secret operation it remains ineffable, incomprehensi-
ble and indefinable. It has been conceived of as the
divine Logos, the Word...[38]

"The Word" alluded to in the passage above from the *Zohar* is
the will of God as the *primal vibration* or energy fluctuation that
"moved upon the face of the waters." It contains all vibrations and
tones. It is "God's voice" speaking God's name—"I AM"—in an
act of divine self-realization and self-affirmation. From *The Word,*
all motion, activity and life processes began. As the *Zohar* further
proclaims: "It produced and impressed a wave-like motion
throughout the boundless ether in which were contained all the
sounds of the alphabet," or all the frequencies of the microcosmic
vibrating strings from which the universe is theorized to be constructed.[39]

In an alphabetic written language, words are comprised of
orderly arrangements of letters. In the physical universe, matter is
made up of an orderly arrangement of sub-atomic particles. Could
it be that each letter in that cosmic alphabet of *The Word* of creation corresponds to a distinct sub-atomic particle or fundamental
force in the Universe? It is interesting to note, according to
Professor Greene, a sub-atomic particle is not really point-like but
"is comprised of a vibrating, dancing filament that physicists have
named a string."[40] Apparently, the physical universe (including all
matter, energies, and forces), at the most microscopic level, "is
unified under the same rubric of microscopic string oscillations—

the 'notes' that strings can play" or the notes the voice of the Creator can speak.[41]

Could it be that these vibrating strings that are the essence of all matter, energies, and forces in the physical universe, are sounding forth *The Word of God (Ohm)* throughout the Cosmos of Manifest Existence? And if this is true, what is the underlying message being sung from the deepest constituent particles of all matter throughout the vast spaces between particles, star systems, and galaxies, in all dimensions and throughout the eons of time? As the works of every artist reflect the unique personality of their creator and often bear the signature of the artist, shouldn't we expect the unique identifying imprint of the "Artist of the Cosmos" to be implanted within that artist's creative progeny? And what name would one expect to hear within the identifying message? Perhaps the name given to Moses by God on Mount Sinai—I AM that I AM."

We realize we are asking challenging questions at the leading edge of current human understanding. We are aware that such questions require a revisitation, reassessment and reintegration of scientific disciplines, philosophical conceptions, and theological belief systems. But these are necessary avenues of inquiry that scientists have been loath to address since Descartes established distinct boundaries segregating theology and science.

Descartes' profoundly insightful statement, "I think, therefore I am" is a simple, elegant expression of self-aware consciousness and self-affirmation. The probing mind begs to inquire from whence arose this consciousness that thinks and is aware of its doing so. Is there something inherent in matter and the understood laws of science that can explain the origin of the phenomenon of self-aware consciousness in entities we define to be living? Is it in the nature of flesh to think or of bones to reason? Does consciousness arise spontaneously from inanimate matter or does the existence of individualized consciousness imply the existence of a deeper intrinsic source of that consciousness? These questions may serve as the rendezvous for open-minded scientists, philosophers, and theologians to engage in a meaningful and mutually-respectful exchange of views in a manner that embraces all scientific evidence and human empirical experience. An honest and humble sharing of insights among scholars and mystics may provide humanity a more enlightened outlook on the universe, our place within it, and how human beings can live healthier and more fulfilling lives.

In the chapters that follow, we will explore further the *Divine Signature* or *fingerprints of identity* as they reveal themselves in the principles and characteristics of living systems, of ourselves, and of *The Many*.

Chapter 6

The Signature of Creation

"Now the Voice that originated from my Thought exists as three permanences: the Father, the Mother, the Son... it (Voice) has within it a Word endowed with every [glory], and it has three masculinities, three powers, and three names. They exist in the manner of Three □□□ — which are quadrangles — secretly within the silence of the Ineffable One."

From one of the early *Christian Nag Hammadi* texts:
Trimorphic Protennoia, XIII 35, 1–50, [24]

Three as one

According to many mystical traditions, three primary qualities of *The One* initiated and directed the initial act of creation. These qualities continue to influence and direct, as fundamental creative principles, all subsequent creative activity and "profoundly affect the nature of the Universe."[1] They are, in a sense, the "Holy Trinity" of creative intelligence that has become the distinctive signature of *The One* implanted throughout the creative masterpiece of the universe identifying the unique beingness of this Supreme Artist of the Cosmos. The *Tao Te Ching* refers to them when it states, "The Tao begot One. One begot Two. Two begot Three. And Three begot the ten thousand things."[2] These three creative qualities are epitomized in the *I-Ching* by the basic structure of the trigram (the fundamental component of the sixty-four divining hexagrams of change).*(Figure 6-1)* The Kabbalistic texts refer to these creative qualities as the "Zahzot" or the "Three Hidden Splendors." In the *Zefer Yetzirah,* the Kabbalistic *Book of Creation,* they are the three books with which God created the universe: "And He created His universe with three books (Sepfarim); with text (Sepher), with number (Sephar), and with communication (Sippur)."[3] Linguistically, they are analogous to the preposition, noun and verb. Geometrically, they are represented as the point, circle, and line. Biologically, they may manifest as the "triplet coding" of DNA and RNA by which the proteins of life are made in every cell. (Like the *I-Ching,* there are sixty-four possible combinations of triplet codes in DNA that code for the basic proteins of all life on this planet.) With respect to the light of consciousness, they create the light and, in turn, are embodied by it because they are hidden within it (hence, they are "Hidden Splendors") as the three primary colors of light (bluish-violet, green, and red) are hidden within the light of the sun. They are the three cardinal archetypes of creation and are often represented by the triscele.*(Fig. 6-2)*

Fig. 6-1. (right) The 64 hexagrams of the I Ching from the Chinese Book of Changes. The I Ching has been used in China since approximately 1000 B.C. for divining the wisest action to take regarding the future outcome of a particular event. The 64 hexagrams are formed by a permutation of the yin and yang trigrams. The underlying principle of the I Ching is based on the Taoist belief that the universe is created and sustained by the constant interplay of two primary, complementary forces — the female and passive yin and the masculine and active yang.

Fig. 6-2. (left) Triscele or Triskelion: A common motif in ancient Celtic art. It is an archetypal symbol of power and the dynamic energy of creation. It was called the "Secret Fire" by alchemists and represents the "Three Creative Principles" of the trinity, acting as "The One."

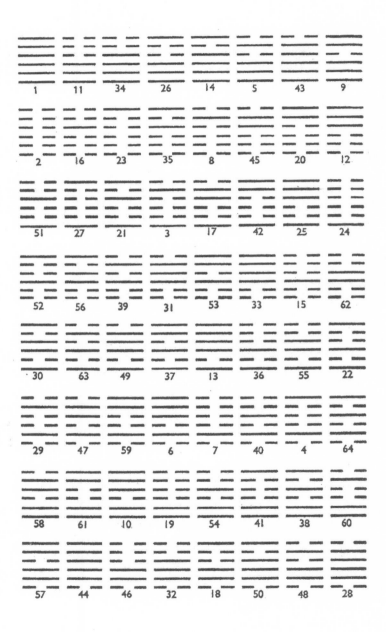

We believe these three principles are more easily conceptualized in the teachings of the late mystic educator Edna Lister.[4] She referred to them as "Mind," "Substance" and "Power" and recognized them as being experienced in a person's everyday life as "Thinking," "Imagination" and "Desire" respectively. These principles can be described in greater detail as follows:

Mind *(Consciousness)*

Mind, as consciousness, represents the organizing aspect inherent in energy and matter that *in*forms (instructs) and *en*forms (constructs) the potential of energy/matter ultimately resulting in Form. It is the "design concept" or "intentional cause" of a thing, and directs the pattern of that object's organization and development. In our opinion, it is this principle the late physicist David Bohm referred to as the "implicate order" that is implied in the phenomenon of matter and may well be likened to a "field of consciousness" or a "quantum field" as described in modern physics.[5] As with a quantum field, Mind conceptually configures the pattern of relationships among matter's elementary particles, ultimately determining the potential form and structure of matter. Mind is enacted through matter by the power of will. Mystically and mythologically, Mind is associated with wisdom—the seed within the womb. Linguistically, it is the preposition. Geometrically, it is the point—the undefined, dimensionless locus. Mind's associated primary color of light is bluish-violet. Its associated primary color of pigment is yellow. In primary Judeo-Christian concepts it might be referred to as "God the Father."

Substance *(Matter)*

Substance, as matter, is *in*formed and *en*formed by Mind to become the embodiment of Mind's pattern of form, resulting in "structure." As Mind informs substance of the pattern of form, it collapses the potential of substance's non-local waveform, thereby enforming it into the local reality of particle manifestation. Mystically and mythologically, Substance is associated with love and the womb, the ocean, and the earth, because Substance is receptive and malleable to the action of Mind through the Power of Will, and it surrenders itself to be embodied by form. Mystically, this quality is said to entice Mind into acting upon it. Linguistically, Substance is the noun. Geometrically, it is the circle. Its associated primary color of light is green. Its associated primary color of pigment is blue. In primary Christian concepts it might be referred to as "The Holy Spirit."

Power *(Energy)*

Power, as energy, is associated with will and the forces that have the ability to act upon matter (electromagnetism, gravity, the strong and weak nuclear forces). This quality constitutes the informing and enforming action of Mind on Matter. It is the power or action of will. It is the creative impulse of *The One*. Mystically and mythologically, Power is associated with passion, desire, joy, and the acts of conception and fertilization. Power catalyzes, sets into motion, and maintains the continued embodiment of Mind within Substance, of the pattern of consciousness within matter. This is the principle that underlies the expression of desire, ambition, achievement, sexuality, and creativity. Linguistically, Power is the verb. Geometrically, Power is the line (radius) that establishes, defines, and maintains the relationship between the point (Mind) and the circle (Substance) and traces the vector of Mind's unfolding. Power's associated primary color of light and pigment is red. In primary Christian concepts it might be referred to as "the blood of the lamb" and/or "God the Son."

As the pure essence of *The One* hidden within the "light of consciousness," these three creative principles are thought to permeate the Womb of Creation. The manifest universe is made of this pure essence, solidified initially by the Deific Mind into the galaxies and star systems of the known universe and modified by individualized consciousnesses across the Cosmos. As quantized units of self-aware consciousness collaborating in the creative process, we have the power of will through free choice to impress upon this primordial essence the potential design intentions conceived by the individualized and collective Mind.

All creative activity takes place through these three cardinal principles. For example, if you wanted to make a cake, you would first have to know what a cake is, what it looks like, and how to make one. The concept of "cake" and the recipe for producing it are manifestations of Mind. Next, you would need the ingredients to make the cake. These materials are manifestations of the principle of Substance or matter. But recipe and ingredients do not produce a cake in and of themselves. The ingredients must be measured, blended, and baked according to the recipe. The action or directed energy expenditure to combine materials in the pattern of the recipe and the heat required for baking is an expression of the principle of Power as directed energy or will. This simple situation exemplifies the application of these three principles in everyday life. Ultimately, in order to create anything, you need the harmonious expression of these three principles. You need to know what it is you are creating (its pattern of organization or form). You need to have the materials necessary to make it (the substance to embody the pattern or form). And finally, you need the action of applying the pattern to the materials to consciously direct energy and activity toward bringing the pattern into fruition. In other words, you need the will or desire to do it and the associated action to make it so.

All creative activity takes place through the three creative principles of Mind, Power and Substance.

When described in the above manner, the appearance of these principles in daily life may seem intuitively obvious and easily understood. What is unknown to many and applied by few, is the fact that these creative principles are operative on all levels, even subconsciously. In order for you to experience your desires, for Substance to conform to the intended pattern of manifestation created by the Mind, that pattern must be absolutely clear and unambiguous while the Power of Will (desire) remains persistent and unwavering. Any failing on your part to maintain clarity of vision, intended purpose and perseverance of desire in action, will prevent or impede the manifestation of the desired outcome. You may intend consciously for the Universe to manifest a certain desired result; but if there are subconscious thoughts, beliefs and fears that oppose the conscious purpose, the desired outcome is thwarted.

All thoughts, beliefs, and ideas, conscious and sub-conscious, are creative. They establish a pattern and consistency of manifestation commensurate with the intensity with which an individual or group holds them as truths. Thus, we must all be diligently careful in the thoughts we choose to hold dear because we create our own realities and the realities of our various societies and cultures. Be careful what you ask for because you just might get it!

The three creative principles are totally interdependent and cannot be separated. Not one of them acts alone. They act as one. Each one is implied in the others. From their coordinated interaction through the reflective, recursive cycle of living systems, life creates, organizes, maintains, and evolves itself. We call these creative principles features of creative intelligence that are the personality characteristics or fingerprint of *The One*. They are what physicist Fritjof Capra refers to as "the key criteria of a living system." In other words, they are the criteria one applies to a system to determine whether it is living.[6]

The three creative principles are totally interdependent and cannot be separated. Not one of them acts alone. They act as one.

In his book *The Web of Life,* Capra describes these three "key criteria of a living system" as follows:

- *Pattern of Organization:* "configuration of relationships of the parts"

- *Structure:* "physical embodiment of the pattern of organization"

- *Life Process:* "activity involved in maintaining the continued embodiment of the pattern of organization"

The *pattern of organization* is "the configuration of relationships that determine the system's essential characteristics" and is mystically associated with the creative principle of Mind.[7] According to Capra, the pattern of organization of a system also determines whether that system is living or nonliving. According to the latest theory of living systems, he calls the intrinsic ability of a system to maintain its pattern of organization "the defining characteristic of life." He further defines *structure* as "the physical embodiment of the system's pattern of organization" and *life process* as "the activity involved in the continual embodiment of the system's pattern of organization."[8] We believe these three key criteria of a living system—pattern of organization, structure and life process—are synonymous with the Three Hidden Splendors as described at the beginning of this chapter. These criteria or principles are embodied in the phenomenon called *autopoiesis.*[9]

The three creative principles are embodied in autopoiesis.

Autopoiesis and continuous creation

Autopoiesis is a term that literally means "self–making." An autopoietic system is a system that "makes itself." Autopoiesis is associated with living systems because *living systems continually produce themselves.* They do this by generating and sustaining structures that perpetuate their pattern of organization. Autopoiesis is also synonymous with continuous creation—the seed that produces the tree that makes the fruit that contains the seed that produces the tree and so on.

As you may recall, continuous creation is the outcome of the self-reflective, iterative process established by the outside-in, inside-out model of original creation—the 3, 10 torus knot of the dimpled spheroid. We suggest this is the organizational pattern modeled by all living systems. The presence of this self-reflective, self-iterative process suggests autopoiesis and may be the necessary and sufficient criterion to designate a system as being "alive." Its presence may determine life. The establishment and continued embodiment of this pattern in a living system is completely dependent upon the directing and organizing action of consciousness upon matter (Mind upon Substance) fueled by the continued input of energy as will. In other words, the organizational pattern of life must be maintained by a continuous effort in harmony with the Three Hidden Splendors of Creative Intelligence which are the "three key criteria" for a living system to continually produce itself.

Living systems embody autopoiesis because
living systems continually produce themselves.

The term "autopoiesis" was coined by Humberto Maturana, Ph.D., and Fransisco Varela, Ph.D., in their attempt to describe more accurately the process of circular organization within systems.[10] According to their pioneering research in the fields of cybernetics, neuroscience and systems theory, the ability of a system or network to produce itself continually is a key criterion for it to be considered as living.[11] Because of the organizational similarities or symmetry observed between the pattern of organization required for autopoiesis and the pattern of organization required for the development of cognitive functions in cybernetics and neuroscience, Maturana and Varela have also suggested that autopoiesis and cognition (mind) are two different aspects of the same phenomenon of life.[12] Does this mean that autopoiesis is a function or aspect of consciousness? If we accept the theory of structural coherence (The structural features or pattern of organization of a system correspond directly to the structural features of its consciousness.), as proposed by David Chalmers, Ph.D, the answer to this question may be yes.[13]

According to Chalmers, "There are deep and fundamental ties between consciousness and cognition."[14] Essentially, where there is cognition there is consciousness. If this is so, the suggestion by Maturana and Varela that autopoiesis and cognition (mind) are two different aspects of the same phenomenon of life supports the concept that life and consciousness are synonymous. Autopoiesis infers life and the pattern of organization required for autopoiesis infers consciousness.

Autopoiesis:

- Autopoiesis (the ability of a system or network to produce itself continually) is a key criterion for a system or network to be considered as living.

- Autopoiesis and consciousness are two different aspects of the same phenomenon of life.

- The pattern of organization required for autopoiesis is very much like the pattern of organization required for consciousness and cognitive functions.

- The presence of autopoiesis infers the presence of consciousness.

- The self-reflective (outside-in, inside-out) pattern of organization required for life is very much like the self-reflective pattern of organization required for consciousness.

- Autopoiesis, life and consciousness may be synonymous.

The structural features or pattern of organization of a system, according to Chalmers, correspond directly to the structural features of its consciousness.[15] The material realist might conclude from this idea that consciousness arises from a system's physical pattern of organization as an "epi-phenomenon" of matter. (Matter comes first; then consciousness arises from it.) However, we propose the physical pattern of organization is the result of *consciousness acting through matter.* (Consciousness comes first; then matter arises from it.) In other words, the organizational pattern of life and living systems is the result of consciousness (as the "Spirit" or "Light of God") projecting itself into creation through the three creative principles so that God can behold God. To observe and recognize the organizational pattern of life in all living things is to see the distinctive Face of *The One* in all living things.

Autopoiesis arises from the pattern of organization of a living system. That pattern is one of circular organization and the outside-in, inside-out model of self-reflection. It is, as Capra describes:

> A network pattern in which the function of each
> component participates in the production or transfor-
> mation of other components in the network. In this

> way, the network continually makes itself. It is pro-
> duced by its components and in turn produces those
> components.[16]

This pattern is a result of each component entering into relationship, not only with the other components of the whole, but also with the whole itself. Each component defines the whole and, in turn, is defined by the whole. Each one produces the other because, in reality, there is no "other." There is only *The One*. Imagine a state in which the components of such a network or system are in continual conflict with each other (me vs. you), failing to perceive their contextual relationship with each other and the whole through active communication and cooperation. How functional would such a system be? Obviously, it would quickly breakdown and degenerate.(Is this state not reminiscent of many dysfunctional human organizations— families, communities, nations, etc.?)

Autopoiesis arises from the pattern of organization of a living system. That pattern is one of circular organization and the outside-in, inside-out model of self-reflection and iteration that is the face of God.

An autopoietic system is self-contained and organizationally closed within well-demarcated boundaries. Boundaries clarify domain and define a system as a unit, as a "self." A system's boundaries are determined by two elements. The first more static, defining and quantifiable element is the physical extent of the systems organizational pattern—the boundaries of a system's *physical structure*. The second more dynamic, mutable and intangible element is the extent of a system's *influence* or *effect* on its environment beyond its physical or structural boundaries. The first element corresponds to the symmetry of a *thing*—its physical body or container—which is metaphorically associated with the circle, womb, or particle of matter. The second element corresponds to the asymmetry of *process*—its mind or consciousness—which is metaphorically associated with the point, seed or wave function of light.

Generally, in the physical realm, human consciousness perceives asymmetry to be contained within symmetry. (The mind is contained within the *body* or consciousness is contained within the organizational pattern of a living system.) However, because of the paradoxical nature of self-reflection and the outside-in, inside-out recursive model of living systems, the opposite is also true relative to the moment and the situation. The asymmetry of consciousness can project beyond the symmetry of its container to influence and affect the world outside of itself. Symmetry and asymmetry co-exist within each other, as order co-exists within chaos and chaos within order.

Although an autopoietic system is self-contained and organizationally closed, it interacts with its external environment through a continual exchange and bi-directional flow of energy and matter. In this regard, an autopoietic system is an "open system," as opposed to a "closed system." Remember, as we discussed earlier, that all living systems take in the outer world, process it in some manner, and give it back transformed. Whether it is food processed by digestion, a seed processed by germination, or an experience processed by the mind, an autopoietic system must always be an open system interacting with the external environment in order for that system to be a living system engaged in continuous creation.

An autopoietic system is an open system.

As we discussed earlier, this process of taking in the outer world, acting on it, and giving it back transformed is the process of consciousness and of life. It incorporates autopoiesis while the phenomenon of autopoiesis, in turn, embodies the aspect of Mind or consciousness. Autopoiesis therefore, insinuates the presence of conscious design and, as Maturana and Varela suggest, the possibility that all living systems manifest some form of consciousness and cognitive phenomena.[17] In consideration of this fact and all we have presented up to this point, we suggest *consciousness, life and God are synonymous.*

The pattern of organization that determines life also appears to be the pattern of organization that determines consciousness. This pattern may be the definitive tangible manifestation of *The One's* identity and the best evidence of conscious design behind the creation of the universe. It may also provide the most sapient criteria upon which one can clearly define health and better understand the healing process and underlying causes of illness.

Let us take a moment to summarize what we have discussed about the organizational pattern of life and living systems up to this point.

First summary of living systems

- All living systems are defined by a unique pattern of organization, which determines their identity.

- All living systems display a circular, recursive, self-reflective pattern of organization based on the original outside-in, inside-out self-referential model of creation.

- All living systems are contextually defined and maintain their unique pattern of organization by:

    1) A continual dialogue of informational exchange between each component of the system with the

other components and with the whole through a network pattern of feedback loops.

2) A continual bidirectional exchange of energy, matter, and experiential phenomena with the external environment.

3) The continued ordering action of consciousness within matter actualized and maintained (by the power of will as energy) through the Three Hidden Splendors of Creative Intelligence.

- By virtue of their circular, recursive, self-reflective pattern of organization:

1) All living systems self-organize and self-regulate through a network pattern of circular, recursive feedback loops based on iteration in which each component of the network participates in the production and transformation of the other components and of the system as a whole.

2) All living systems take in the outside world in some form, process it, and then give it back again changed and transformed in some way.

3) All living systems are autopoietic and continually self-organize, self-regulate, grow, adapt, evolve and self-replicate.

4) All living systems display some degree of consciousness and creative intelligence by virtue of their unique pattern of organization.

Chapter 7

Archetypes of Nature and the Pattern of Life

> *"Life processes include two basic elements: self-identity and self-alteration (growth). A central and balanced living whole goes beyond itself parting from its unity, but in doing so it tries to preserve its identity and to return in its separated parts to itself. Going out from one's self characterizes life under all dimensions, from the structure of the atom to the growth of the plant, to the movement of the animal, to the creativity of the mind, to the dynamics of historical groups. One can call this dialectics of life processes because it implies contrasting movements, a yes and a no, as in searching conversation."*

Paul Tillich from *The Meaning of Health*, 1981

Archetypes of pattern

The early Greek philosophers Pythagoras and Plato believed the universe was ordered according to fundamental harmonic and mathematical principles. Plato referred to these principles as the "absolute Ideas" held in the mind of the One Supreme Intelligence or Creator. He believed these Ideas generated the ideal or rational Forms that are the governing but hidden truths of the temporal, experiential, material world. Aristotle further suggested that the substance of this material world is given its essential shape, structure, distinctive essence and developmental dynamic by the Forms embodied in it (spirit embodied in matter). This thinking underlies the concept of archetype. However, modern conceptual models of the universe have been, for the most part, devoid of such thinking.

Over the past few centuries, the scientific community has focused most of its attention upon the phenomena of energy and matter. Pattern, form and the abstract phenomenon of Mind or consciousness have generally been ignored. The investigational emphasis on energy and matter, rather than form and pattern, may have been due to the fact that energy and matter were historically readily experienced through the senses and more easily quantified. They were also more subject to conceptual modeling and mathematical analysis through linear equations, while only the simplest of forms (those remaining static and unchanging) presented the possibility of being represented by linear mathematical expression. Living forms do not behave in a manner convenient to simple linear analysis, however. They present mathematical challenges of notable complexity. Then there is the question of Mind or consciousness. It is so intangible scientists can't even agree yet that it even exists. And how would it ever be quantified?

The natural patterns and forms of living systems are not static. They are dynamic, metamorphic and at times asymmetric. They constantly undergo transformation and reorganization into greater expressions of complexity and diversity. A different type of mathematical tool than linear equations is called for when analyzing, describing and modeling such natural forms. The analysis and description of living forms requires the use of nonlinear equations. Through the application of nonlinear mathematics, these dynamic, complex forms are only now beginning to be understood. This inquiry has yielded a new understanding of the organizational pattern of living systems and has also led to an intriguing fascination with chaos.

The natural patterns and forms of living systems are *dynamic, metamorphic* and at times *asymmetric.* When not entropic, they constantly undergo transformation and reorganization into greater expressions of complexity and diversity.

The non-linear approach may offer new insights into heretofore baffling questions regarding form:

- Why has a particular form or pattern evolved for any particular living entity?

- Why do atomic particles, atoms, and molecules combine repeatedly and predictably in patterns that generate the chemical structures of matter?

- How are DNA molecules, proteinaceous compounds, and cellular entities guided to form the diverse tissues of complex living organisms? How are cells directed to produce a leg instead of an arm, or a flower instead of a butterfly?

- Why are planets shaped as spheroids and galaxies in the configuration of spirals?

- What dictates the patterns of form, and how is that pattern imposed upon matter?

The answers to these questions may lie in modern field theory and the study of chaos viewed from the perspective of the ancient concept of *archetypal forms.* Archetypes are the fundamental forms or patterns from which all complex forms are derived. In modern field theory, fields are primary and underlie the forms and shapes of material bodies as well as the space between them. Fields, like archetypes, act as the organizing aspect of consciousness and represent the quality of Mind. According to Rupert Sheldrake, Ph.D., proponent of the theory of *morphic resonance,* "Physical phenomena are explained by a combination of the concepts of spatial fields and of energy, not in terms of energy alone."[1] Is this just another way of saying physical phenomena are explained by the organizing action of Mind upon Substance through the Power of will? Sheldrake goes on to say:

> Although energy can be regarded as the cause of change, the ordering of change depends on the spatial structure of the fields. These structures have physical effects, but they are not in themselves a type of energy; they act as 'geometrical' or spatial causes.[2]

We suggest the "geometrical" or "spatial causes" referred to by Sheldrake may be the effects of consciousness or the aspect of Mind acting through matter to *en*form the physical universe.

Acting as the organizing aspect of consciousness, fields, like archetypes, are primary and underlie the forms and shapes of material bodies as well as the space between them.

The most fundamental of fields, according to theoretical physicist Henning Genz, is the "Higgs Field."[3] It is proposed to be the very first field that appeared within the Void (the Womb of Creation) at the beginning of the universe and which has pervaded the entire empty space of the universe ever since. Below a certain very high temperature, only achieved at the moment of the original creation or Big Bang, "the Higgs field can, and indeed must, appear out of the void."[4] It distinguishes and dictates certain directions, geometrical patterning, and spatial causes within its own abstract space spanned by the properties of elementary particles. As these elementary particles of matter spontaneously manifest, they follow the patterning of the field's directives in both behavior and form. These "directives" or "spatial causes" of the Higgs Field may be the original and fundamental patterns or organizing principles—the archetypes—from which all subsequent forms and patterns of organization have evolved.

The great French mathematician and astronomer Pierre Simon de Laplace (1749–1827) believed that all the effects of nature are only the mathematical consequences of a small number of immutable laws. We suggest that the spatial structures or geometric patterns embodied in the primal field are the geometrical expressions of these immutable laws, (i.e., *the archetypes of forms*). We further suggest that the field phenomenon itself is the functional outcome of the principle of Mind as we discussed previously. Taking this into consideration, one might further propose the possibility that a field is the physical manifestation of the consciousness of *The One* informing and enforming matter through the immutable laws of *The One's* own nature with the patterns of organization (fingerprints of *One's* identity) that have and continue to form and shape the created universe.

As artists are known to instill their own identifying characteristics into their creations, the archetypal forms or patterns of organization that have shaped the universe may be the fundamental patterns of *The One's* identity. As such, they may mirror back to the Source (via the outside-in, inside-out self-reflective model of creation) the distinctive features of *The One's* multi-faceted "Face"—the Face of God. It can then be said that each archetype represents a fundamental deific characteristic of *The One* that must be expressed in order for *The One* to behold and realize Itself.

Obsessed with order, Pythagoras and Plato considered five geometric solids to be the primary or archetypal forms of creation in an ordered linear universe. Known as the "perfect solids" or the "Platonic solids," these forms are the cube, octahedron, tetrahedron, dodecahedron, and icosahedron. *(See Fig. 2-2)* The concept of these solids as primal was based on the belief that the Universe was perfectly ordered and symmetrical. The perfect solids meet within each solid, specific criteria: all edges are of equal length, all angles are equal, all surfaces are identical, and all the points of each solid touch the surface of a surrounding sphere. This last criteria, however, makes the circle and sphere even more fundamental. Therefore, mathematically and structurally, in the linear realm of perfect symmetry and order, the circle and sphere are the most fundamental of geometric forms, preceded only in simplicity by the line and the point from which they are constructed. Therefore, the point, line and circle/sphere are the primary archetypes of form in an ordered material universe. But in the more chaotic realm of dynamical systems and transformational change (the real world of nature, living systems, and the domain of process) the spiral transcendently replaces the circle. *(See Fig. 7-1)*

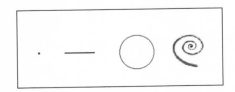

Fig. 7-1. The point, line, circle/sphere and spiral.

The spiral is the circle in a state of transforming, dynamic process. It incorporates and symbolizes the outside-in, inside-out enfolding and unfolding process of creation, while expressing the cyclic, eternal nature of the circle. This may be why the DNA molecule at the center of every cell, representing the central point of dynamic process in the original spiraling vortex of creation, is shaped as a spiral or double helix.[5]

In the world of symmetry, the circle and sphere are the most fundamental of geometric archetypal forms preceded only in simplicity by the line and the point.

In the world of *asymmetry*, the spiral is the most fundamental of geometric archetypal forms preceded only in simplicity by the line and the point.

It is postulated that all the forms and patterns of nature are progressively more complex variations of the fundamental archetypes of creation, continuously revealing the nature and identity of *The One*. Of these archetypes, the circle/sphere (in the realm of structure), the spiral (in the realm of process), the line, and the point are most primal. From these archetypes, all form and structure can be generated.[6]

All the forms and patterns of nature are progressively more complex variations of the primary archetypes of creation: The point, line, circle/sphere (realm of structure), and spiral (realm of process).

The point

All directions (up, down, sideways, north, south, east, west, etc.), dimensions (length, width, height, depth), measurements, mathematical principles, and geometrical constructs begin with a point. However, drawing a true point is impossible, because a true point is absolutely dimensionless. In truth, it does not exist except in our conceptual reality. It has no length, width, height or depth. It expresses no duality, opposites or contrasts. It simply *is* and *is not*. As the "atractor point" at the center of the spiraling vortex, it is at the heart of the flow where the exterior is drawn into the interior or the interior unfolds out to the exterior. Kabbalistically and mystically, the point represents *aleph,* the first letter of the Hebrew alphabet and the "first cause." It is the "divine singularity" or "divine seed" from which the Cosmos arises. It was the seed point in the womb of the void at the beginning of creation. It is both the "Alpha" and the "Omega"—the Beginning and the Ending— because it is the perfect state in which the opposites are united. As the beginning of everything, the point is singular because the opposites have not yet been created or separated. As the end, it is singular because the opposites have been re-joined in perfect unity and synthesis so that the universe is once again at rest. As mathematician Michael Schneider, describes it:

> "The point is the source of our whole of wholes. It is beyond understanding, unknowable, silently self-enfolded. But like a seed, a point will expand to fulfill itself as a circle."[7]

The circle/spiral

If the point is "aleph," then the circle or spiral into which it expands to fulfill itself is *beth*. *Beth* is the second letter of the Hebrew alphabet. According to Kabbalistic tradition, this is the letter from which creation began in the original Hebrew biblical text, because it is the first letter of the first word (*"B'rashit"*) of

Biblical Genesis. It represents the container or maternal womb within which creation takes place.

The circle and spiral present the maximal contrast of inside and outside, finite and infinite. They intimate the ultimate paradox: They are simultaneously limiting in their ability to contain and define, yet unlimiting and endless in their dimensions (Π=3.1415926...) and their expansive, recursive nature. Perceived as the uroboros (the ancient symbol of the serpent swallowing its tail), the circle is the symbol of unity and eternity, the union of masculine and feminine opposites as the mythological "World Parents" joined in perpetual embrace. As Michael Schneider states, "... a circle implies the mysterious generation from nothing to everything."[8] While the circle accommodates all of the fundamental two-dimensional shapes within itself and the sphere accommodates all of the fundamental three-dimensional forms (Platonic solids) within itself, *the spiral accommodates the primary creative process* from which all the fundamental shapes and forms evolve.

All forms and organizing patterns of life arise from the spiral, circle, and sphere. Within them lies the identity of the Creator. Understanding them allows you to understand yourself because it is from them you were born. Discover and explore the many sacred circles (mandalas) and spirals that are part of numerous mythological, theological and mystical traditions. Contemplate them and meditate on them. They can be a source of revelation about your true identity and the identity of your Creator. As Neumann states:

> "So long as man shall exist, perfection will con-
> tinue to appear as the circle, the sphere, and the
> round; and the Primal Deity who is sufficient unto
> himself, and the self who has gone beyond the oppo-
> sites, will reappear in the image of the round, the
> mandala."[9]

The line

Finally, there is the line. A line establishes a connection or relationship between two distinct points and reveals direction of movement. Without it there would be no circle or sphere because there would be no radius to define circumference or surface. There would be no direction of movement, maximal contrast or polarity, and no linear continuum. The experience of separation is dependent on the line because of the line's ability to "cut through" and divide. Yet, as the linear continuum of infinity, the line represents both the polarity of opposite directions and the connector that joins them. Mystically, it expresses the will of *The One* that draws all into relationship. The line, as the radius, expands from the Divine Singularity of the central point to the outer manifestation of the circle, which is the circumference of all there is. The line draws and directs the exterior to the interior and vice versa. It represents the oppositional and contrasting, primal and eternal movement of contraction and expansion, inhalation and exhalation, enfolding and unfolding.

As we have stated, all the complex organizational patterns of living systems are based on simple circular, self-reflective, spiraling themes of recursion and iteration rooted in the primary principle of maximal contrast and polarity. These patterns are initiated and directed by the Three Hidden Splendors of creation as they are represented in form by the point, the spiral/circle and the line. However, the characteristics and behavior of these simple circular, spiraling themes have pushed scientists out of the comfortable, ordered realm of the "perfect solids," Platonic harmonies and Newtonian linear mechanics into the unsettling realm of nonlinearity, chaos theory, and fractal geometry.[10]

Archetypes of process

In nature, nonlinear systems with their spiraling, recursive, continuous, and oftentimes abrupt and dramatic, change through chaos are the norm; the gradually changing, orderly, linear systems, with which the human intellect is most comfortable, are more commonly aberrations from the norm. The dynamic phenomena of chaos and nonlinearity are characteristic of the true nature of nature. If the point, the circle/sphere, and the line are the archetypes of form that determine form's pattern of organization, then nonlinearity, chaos, and transformational change (represented by the spiral) are the archetypes of process that direct the unfolding of form. Chaos and nonlinearity transport us into the world of qualities, probabilities, relationships, and choice where we are "liberated" from the limiting, mechanistic world of quantities and deterministic absolutes. Chaos and nonlinearity color and richly landscape our life experience with the anticipatory sensuality of free choice and unexpected transformational change. They are the reality of life and not its abstraction.

Nonlinear functions are crucial to life. They allow microscopic changes within a system to produce dramatic and far-reaching results through spiraling recursion and repeated amplification or *iteration*. Iteration is fundamental to all living systems because it is absolutely essential for the process of growth and evolution, as self-reflection is essential to the unfolding of identity. In nonlinear systems, such as living systems, iteration occurs through feedback loops that cause simple phenomena to evolve great variety, diversity, and richness, while allowing complex chaotic functions to reveal subtler, deeper patterns of order. These nonlinear feedback loops produce periodic instabilities in living systems. These instabilities induce temporary chaos out of which new levels of order and complexity abruptly emerge. This "transformation through chaos" generated by *feedback loops* enables a living system to continually grow and evolve. Iteration and feedback loops are a result and fuction of relationship. They occur as the interaction of two or more things that have entered into relationship with one another.

> Nonlinear functions are crucial to life, because
> they allow microscopic changes within a system
> to produce dramatic and far-reaching results
> through recursion and iteration.

> Continued self-reflection through recursion
> and iteration is absolutely essential for the growth
> and evolution of living systems, and occurs only
> through relationship.

The fractal geometry of self-similarity

Through continual self-reflection via recursion and iteration, the symmetry of self-similarity has been established and maintained in nature. Recursion and iteration have resulted in the unfolding of *The One* into the many through repeated patterning—pattern inside of pattern inside of pattern—like the traditional Russian dolls; one inside of the other. This means the same transformational process is repeated at smaller and smaller or larger and larger scales following the archetypal patterning dictated by the Three Hidden Splendors, the fingerprint of *The One's* identity. Self-similarity is built into the process of continual creation and is a powerful way of generating shape.[11] It is an easily recognizable quality in nature if one would only look. The geometry of self-similarity can be seen everywhere: in a seed, a leaf, a stream, a cloud, a mountain, or a spinning galaxy. It is the geometry of nonlinearity and fractional dimensions exemplified by "fractals." *(See Figs. 7-2 & 7-3 and search fractals online.)*

Fig. 7-2 & 7-3. Fractal illustrations courtesy of Julian Sprott, Ph.D.

French mathematician Benoit Mandelbrot pioneered the development of fractals and gave them their name. They are the structurally visible result (Thanks to computers!) of applied non-linear mathematics where, simply put, a number representing a point z is multiplied by itself (iteration/self-reflection) and added to a constant c. The sum of this equation then becomes the new z and the equation is repeated ($z \rightarrow z^2 + c$). Through repeated patterning and iteration, fractals embody the symmetry of self-similarity and continual creation. They reflect infinity and embrace the realms of chaos and nature describing and delineating all the forms and shapes of the natural world.[12]

When randomness or free will is applied to the repeated patterning and unfolding of fractal geometry, freshness and unpredictability are observed. This spontaneity results in the novelty, richness, and diversity characteristic of the natural forms found in the real, living environment experienced by the senses. When the variable of free choice is added to iteration; novelty, serendipity, and diversity result. As Briggs and Peat point out:

> "Fractals become more organic when, at each step, there is choice between several alternative forms of iteration, or when a particular fractal iteration persists for several length scales and then suddenly changes."[13]

Free choice, even in the realm of random fractals, apparently yields greater variety and diversity.

As stated earlier, variety and diversity appear to be cardinal themes in life's continuing story—"prime directives" of *The One's* self-affirmation. On deeper reflection, one can conclude that it could not be otherwise. The variety and diversity of *The Many* in order to express the boundless dimensionality of *The One*, must be vast, beyond the limits of human imagining. Considering this, any attempt to stifle or obstruct the expression of individuality, diversity and deific multiplicity within an individual, a community, or a nation must be an action contrary to life and tantamount to an ungodly act. Certainly, such action must ultimately result in a restriction of creativity and vitality; a restriction of life itself.

Variety and *diversity* through creativity appear to be "prime directives" of The One's self-affirmation.

Self-organization through self-reflection

The essential pattern of a living system is a network pattern of circularly interacting components capable of *self-organization, self-regulation* and *continual creation*. Living systems are made up of networks of interconnected elements with each element having its own characteristics and functions. These elements communicate with each other in a multidirectional fashion, creating a communication web of nonlinear relationships resulting in an integrated, diverse community—a dynamic whole. This communication network generates "feedback loops" and "hypercycles" that play a central role in information feedback (iteration) and response. Feedback, as a function of self-reflection, leads to adjustment of and compensation for any instability or disturbance. How often do you rely on your reflection in a mirror, the opinion of a friend and loved one, or the verbal and nonverbal feedback from a boss, teacher or social environment to influence and direct your behavior and appearance?

The essential pattern of a living system is a network of circularly interacting components capable of self-organization, self-regulation and continual creation due to the presence of nonlinear functions and feedback (iteration).

The outcome of continuous feedback and adjustment in a dynamic system is threefold: *1) homeostasis, 2) self-regulation, and 3) self-organization*. *Homeostasis* is the maintenance of the life-preserving, dynamic, steady-state balance of all elements within a system. The emphasis here should be on "dynamic" because homeostasis is not the passive or static state of equilibrium associated with maximal entropy. In such a static state, the pattern of organization is no longer maintained by a continual intake of energy and the elements of the system break down into a tepid mush of disorganization (nonbeing). Instead, homeostasis is a vigorous active process of constantly adjusting and readjusting to the continuous feedback of external and internal stimuli. This is an energetic, active process that maintains a living system in a state of openness, "far from equilibrium," on the edge of chaos. It is dependent upon a continuous exchange of energy between the system and its environment. It is interesting to note here as well, that dynamic homeostasis has long been considered an important aspect to the definition of health, (i.e., a healthy system is a system in active balance).

The outcome of continuous feedback and adjustment is threefold:

1) self-organization,
2) self-regulation,
3) and homeostasis.

Unobstructed communication among all components of a system is the most essential feature of homeostasis. It assures the integrative wholeness of that system and its ability to self-regulate and self-organize. It arises from a network pattern of organizational relationships (feedback loops and hypercycles) among all elements of the system and infers a bi-directional, "give and take" sharing of information between those elements and the outside world. Without the bi-directional exchange (communication) among all constituents of the system, the interconnectedness of the parts and the consequent integrity or health of the system as a whole can not be maintained. Disruption of this communication would cause internal conflict, disorder, and eventual disintegration of the system and its pattern of organization into the maximal entropy of nonidentity and nonbeing.

Communication within a living system is a function of iteration through feedback loops.[14] *(See Fig. 7-4)* Feedback loops are microcosmic expressions of the very first movement of creation that established the most basic and fundamental pattern of maximal contrast and self-reflection. This pattern is based on the original movement of the creative consciousness of life. It was catalyzed by the primal question of identity (Who/What am I?).

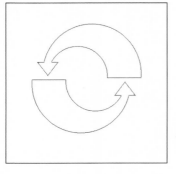

Fig. 7-4. Simple feedback loop.

By the recursive action of iteration and self-reflection, the cosmogonic cycle of life was begun as the first movements of creation (e.g., spin and rotation) were enabled. These motions are vital to the functional characteristics and dynamics of matter (subatomic particles, planets, galaxies, etc.), form and energy (electromagnetism, gravity, etc.). Eventually, iteration and self-reflection established the essential organizational pattern from which life and cognitive functions have developed. Incorporated into biological systems as biochemical and neurological feedback loops and hypercycles, they have enabled the development of cognitive functions in living organisms, making way for the establishment of self-consciousness.[15]

Communication within a living system is a function of iteration through feedback loops and hypercycles.

Evidence suggests that feedback loops manifest spontaneously ("autocatalyze") over time in any open system, no matter how random or disordered its initial state when energy is applied to that system. The origin of life on earth is believed to be the result of multiple feedback loops called hypercycles. Hypercycles have enabled the progressive organization and complexity in chemical systems to develop in energy states far away from passive equilibrium and maximal entropy. The development of hypercycles resulted in the pre-biologic evolutionary process of molecular self-organization. This was accomplished through the generation of chemical reactions capable of self-replication and the correcting of errors in replication. Hypercycles are the means by which chemical systems can evolve into increasingly complex and diverse patterns of order.[16]

Hypercycles:
Self-regulate
Self-organize
Self-reproduce
Evolve

Hypercycles are *self-referring* and *recursive* through the action of feedback loops and "circular organization." These characteristics are essential to the development of cognition, perception, and self-awareness. Remember, as we discussed in Chapter Five, the theoretical reason for all existence is to allow "God to behold God." The "beholding" at a macrocosmic level is accomplished microcosmically by the self-referring and recursive action of hypercycles and feedback loops. They are the cosmogonic cycles of the microcosmic world and are responsible for the self-reflective, iterative character of chemical systems that brought and continue to bring life into physical existence. Most importantly, they are the microcosmic analogue of the "mirror" phenomenon that can be observed at all orders of magnitude in the physical universe. Remember: this self-reflective phenomenon is the means by which "God sees God."

The mirror effect of recursive circular communication is present at all orders of magnitude in the physical universe because it is inherent in the nature of *The One*. This is affirmed in the format of God's name as quoted in Exodus 3:13–14. When Moses encounters God on Mount Sinai as the "burning bush," Moses asks God, "When I come unto the children of Israel, and shall say unto them, The God of your fathers hath sent me unto you; and they shall say to me, What is his name? What shall I say unto them?" God replies, "I AM *that* I AM."[17] [emphasis on the word "that" added]. In our opinion, the word "that," within this name of *The One*, is a linguistic symbol for the cosmic phenomenon that allows Deity to behold Its own Face. "That" is the mirror reflecting the image of "I AM" back to "I AM." We believe this is the reason why the most basic of self-declarative statements— "I AM"—appears twice within the self-proclaimed name of *The One*. "I AM that I AM" may be the most perfect nonlinear equation of being (I AM multiplied by itself then added to the constant of continuous creation) and simplistic model of iteration and self-reflection fundamental to the process of continual creation on all levels of life. It is so simple and yet so profound.

The first "I AM" represents the singular, non-self-aware consciousness of *The One* disseminating its essence into the Void of creative potential to become self-aware. This creative act allows *The One* to manifest, affirm and eventually witness all aspects of Its beingness. Such self-affirming creativity requires self-reflective iteration (feedback) and the illusory experience of separation and maximal contrast to perpetuate the creative processes and achieve self-aware consciousness, as we all need some feedback as to who we are and how we are doing in life. These iterative, self-reflective features of the creative act allow *The One* to express Itself to Itself; and to witness itself through the development of the myriad of diverse forms that *The One* has taken (and will continue to manifest as long as the physical universe exists) since the beginning of time.

"I AM that I AM" may be the most perfect nonlinear equation of being (I AM multiplied by itself then added to the constant of continuous creation) and simplistic model of iteration and self-reflection fundamental to the process of continual creation on all levels of life.

The second "I AM" is *The One* in manifestation as *The Many* and represents the reflected and multiplied image of the first "I AM." This reflection and multiplication allows the consciousness of *The One* to behold Itself and realize Its full identity by gazing upon and experiencing Its magnificently boundless diversity as *The Many*. At the same time, the reflection of the second "I AM" also allows the fully developed egoic consciousness of *The Many* to look to the first "I AM" and "behold the magnificence and glory of the Lord" and proclaim "how excellent is thy name in all the earth who has set thy glory above the heavens."[18]

The word *that,* as it appears in the name of God, is the constant of this self-reflective equation. It is analogous to the act of this observation or witnessing. It is the "mirror of existance" through which God beholds God. It also represents I AM's multiplication of itself into the fractal realization of *The Many*. It is the mirror, the turning point or reflective point at which the circular movement of recursive flow turns back on itself. It is the point where self-aware consciousness in its fullest manifestation and individualized separateness turns back to recognize its source (God as *The Many* beholds God as *The One*). Consciousness beholds its own contextual identity through the relationship of "*The Many* with *The Many*" and "*The Many* with *The One*" (or the relationship of the parts with each other and the parts with the whole). Only through relationship can *The One* know Itself and only through relationship can we know ourselves as individuations of *The One*.

It can be said that the essential purpose of all spiritual practice is the continual reminding of the human ego-mind of where all life and consciousness came from—the conscious turning of ego-mind's focus away from its illusions of the outer, material world and back to its Source, back to The Whole.

The cycle of life and the two deaths of identity

Circular, spiraling, cyclic movement and recursive, iterative flow are characteristic of the most fundamental movements and primal archetypes in the universe. To quote the *Tao Te Ching*, "returning is the motion of the Tao."[19] Cyclic motion represents the circular path from unified, non-self-aware consciousness to individualized self-aware consciousness and then back to the unified, but now self-aware consciousness. Mythologically it is the unending cosmogonic cycle of birth, life experience, death, and rebirth into a new, transformed state. As Joseph Campbell tells us:

> It is to be understood as the passage of universal consciousness from the deep sleep zone of the unmanifest, through dream, to the full day of waking; then back again through dream to the timeless dark. As in the actual experience of every living being, so in the grandiose figure of the living cosmos.[20]

Mystically and mythologically there are two deaths of identity within this cycle. The first death is "banishment," or "separation." It is the death of unindividuated, *non*-self-aware consciousness as it passes from its "paradisal" state of wholeness into the illusory experience of separateness. The second death is the death of ego consciousness or individual identity as it passes from the illusion of separateness into the reality of wholeness again. For the *Unmanifest* to move into the Manifest or the non-self-aware consciousness to become self-aware, these "deaths" are essential and are recapitulated in all levels of living systems.

The Bible symbolically and mythologically presents us with the story of this evolution of self-aware consciousness through these two deaths. The story told in the Old Testament is the story of the journey of egoic consciousness from its paradisal state and bondage in the womb of the unconscious through the trials and tribulations of its exodus into the *Promised Land* of its individuality and self-sufficiency. It is the history and accounting of the journey of the Hebrew people (who symbolically represent the developing ego of self-aware consciousness) out of their bondage and captivity into their freedom of self-identity as a people and as a nation. This journey represents the "first death of identity" on the cycle of life. It is the death from the "paradise consciousness" of unrealized self into the illusory consciousness of separateness.

The history and accounting of the life of Jesus (a descendant of the House of David and the Hebraic lineage), as told in the New Testament, presents us with the further evolution of egoic consciousness. The story of Jesus is the story of the sacrifice, through love and service, of egoic consciousness and its illusion of separateness. It is represented by the second death of identity—the death of the ego—on the cycle of life and the cross of self-sacrifice. Through this sacrificial death, the *I* of egoic consciousness is resurrected into the contextual *Thou* consciousness of self-aware wholeness. From here the consciousness of contextual identity realizes, "I and my Father are one."[21]

The death of paradise consciousness into the illusion of separateness occurs in the first half of the cosmogonic cycle of life (the grand feedback loop of self-aware consciousness) and sets the stage for the development of individual identity and self-awareness *(See Fig. 7-5)*. Theologically it is also represented by the banishment of Adam and Eve from the Garden of Eden because they had "...eaten of the Tree [of Knowledge], whereof I [God] commanded thee that thou shouldest not eat."[22] As we discussed in Chapter Two, when they ate the fruit of that Tree, "the eyes of them both were opened, and they knew that they were naked" and they "hid themselves from the presence of the Lord God."[23] When Adam and Eve ate the fruit, it bestowed upon them the possibility of free choice by giving them the "knowledge of good and evil." In other words, it gave them the ability to perceive and experience

The Cosmogonic Cycle of Life
The Grand Feedback Loop of Self-Aware Consciousness and The First and Second Deaths of Identity

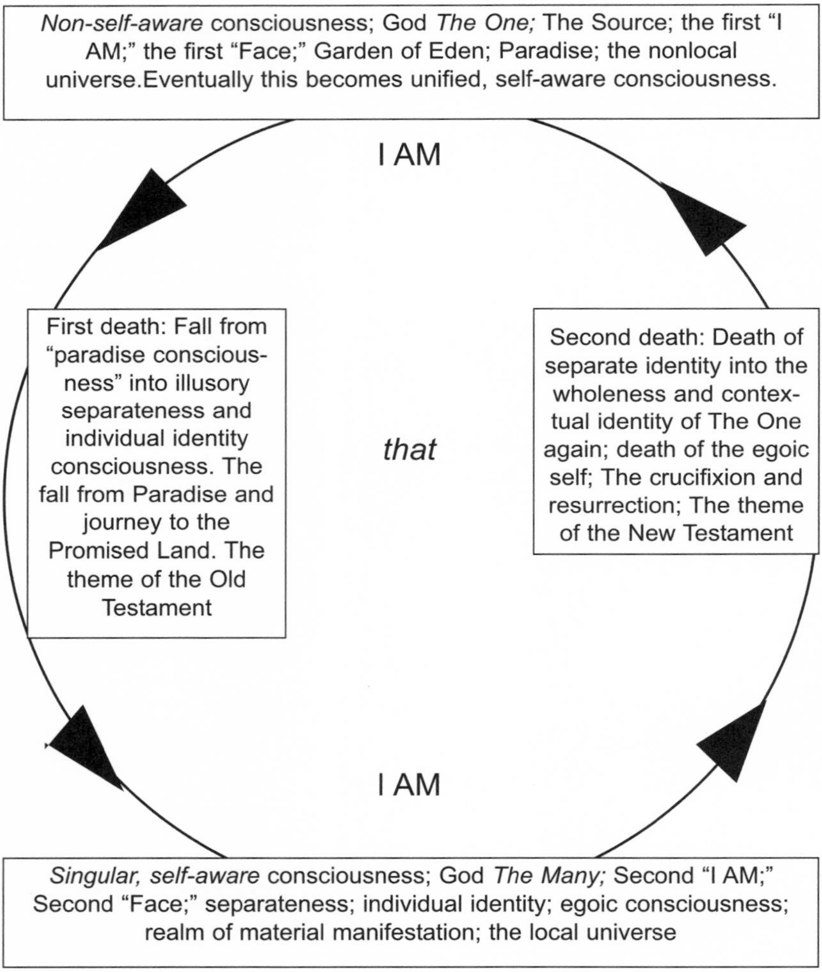

Non-self-aware consciousness; God *The One;* The Source; the first "I AM;" the first "Face;" Garden of Eden; Paradise; the nonlocal universe.Eventually this becomes unified, self-aware consciousness.

I AM

First death: Fall from "paradise conscious- ness" into illusory separateness and individual identity consciousness. The fall from Paradise and journey to the Promised Land. The theme of the Old Testament

that

Second death: Death of separate identity into the wholeness and contex- tual identity of The One again; death of the egoic self; The crucifixion and resurrection; The theme of the New Testament

I AM

Singular, self-aware consciousness; God *The Many;* Second "I AM;" Second "Face;" separateness; individual identity; egoic consciousness; realm of material manifestation; the local universe

Fig. 7-5. The Cosmogonic Cycle of Life

maximal contrast (Good and Evil). This shift in consciousness and perception banished them from the paradise consciousness of integrated wholeness and unrealized self (Garden of Eden) to the illusory consciousness of separateness "where their sorrow would be greatly multiplied."[24]

Keeping with the metaphor of a tree and its fruit, the death of separation can be further represented by the "fruit tree yielding fruit whose seed is in itself."[25] The fruit must be "banished" or separated from the tree, allowing it to fall to the ground so that its seed may bring forth a new tree "after its kind" whose seed is also in itself. (Reproduction within most species requires the separation of pollen or seed from one organism to trigger fertilization within another. This requirement assures relationship.) Without the death of wholeness through separation, individual identity cannot be established. Children must leave home, as the fruit must leave the tree, in order to bring forth new and more diverse expressions and combinations of the many attributes and qualities of *The One*. *The One* must become *The Many* so that *The One* can realize Its own nature through relationship.

The second death, the death of individual identity or egoic consciousness, occurs in the second half of the cosmogonic cycle. Theologically, the crucifixion and resurrection of Jesus represent the second death. Mythologically it is represented by the phoenix rising from the ashes and the Hero's Journey. In nature, it is the death of the caterpillar metamorphosing into a butterfly. It is the fruit, leaves or tree, having fallen to the forest floor, sacrificially propagating the species by rotting in order to fertilize the soil and disseminate the seed. It is also the way of the salmon arduously returning to its birthplace to spawn and then die; sacrificing itself for its offspring and the continuation of its species. This second death is the death of the separate, individualized self and its resulting transformation into the contextual self—the self that is one with all and serves all life. Through this death, one sheds one's illusion of separateness for the reality of wholeness. One "puts forth his hand and takes and eats of The Tree of Life and lives forever."[26] Here the *I* of separateness (the "Lamb of God") is sacrificed on the altar of life in order to embrace the *Thou* of wholeness and become transformed into the truth of life. It is a sacrifice that is programmed expectantly into all living beings but must be consciously chosen by every sentient, self-aware being. It is the mystical journey and experience upon which all religious and theological belief systems are founded. It is also a sacrifice that cannot truly be made unless there is a fully self-realized *I* that is consciously willing to unite with *Thou.*

Section 3:
The Affirmation of Life

Chapter 8

Living on the Edge of Chaos

*"The ambiguity of life exists in every creative process.
In every creative process of life, a destructive trend is implied;
in every integrating process of life, a disintegrating trend;
in every process toward the sublime, a profanizing trend."*

Paul Tillich, Ph.D., from *The Meaning of Health,* 1981

"There is no security in life. There is only opportunity."

General Douglas MacArthur

Staying open to stay alive

The story of life is told and retold over and over through every feedback loop and hypercycle, every birth and death, and every relationship and personal interaction experienced by its vast array of characters from one-celled organisms to humans. Its plot is revealed through life's recurring, circular organizational theme of iteration and self-reflection, enabling each of its characters to self-regulate, self-organize, reproduce (autopoiesis), and function cognitively and consciously eventually to self-transcendance. This recurring theme also enables each character to defy entropy and "passive" equilibrium, allowing each one the ability to establish and maintain a unique, ordered, homeostatic pattern of organization on the edge of chaos in the realm of maximal creativity.[1]

Self-organization is exhibited by a system's ability to:
- Defy the disintegrating influence of entropy and passive equilibrium,
- Spontaneously establish and maintain an ordered pattern of organization in dynamic equilibrium with its environment,
- Spontaneously establish and maintain an ordered pattern of organization on the edge of chaos in the realm of maximal creativity.

Every character in life's continuing story is a living system that must be able to self-organize and self-regulate to exist. This requires each system to be open and able to enter into mutually beneficial relationships with its external environment (the world of non-self). Openness facilitates the continued transformation of a system and its environment. To be open, a system must be able to incorporate into itself useful external energy and matter and be able to process that energy and matter in a self-organizing fashion that sustains and evolves its unique pattern of organization. It must then be able to give that energy and matter back to the external environment transformed in such a way as to influence that environment to make it more hospitable to the system's continued existence. By so doing, *life creates the conditions for its own existence.*

In the evolution of life on our planet, the sun has played the most important role as the primary source of external, low entropy energy for living systems. It has also stood as a primary symbol of

The One and *The One's* life-giving energy because of this. From the sun's energy, the organisms of the primordial biochemical "soup" (algae, bacteria, fungi and, eventually, the higher plants) were able to transform their patterns of organization into progressively more complex integrated structures capable of continual creation. The residue of their transforming life processes (oxygen, organic molecules, nitrogenous wastes, fertile soil, the atmosphere, etc.) eventually changed the earth into a vital, rich and fertile living organism and home for higher, more self-aware life forms. The openness of those primordial organisms to their surroundings, augmented by the creative cleverness of their biochemical adaptability, enabled the earth to self-organize and self-regulate into the complex living ecosystem known as "Gaia"—our "Great Mother Earth."[2]

Life creates the conditions for its own existence.

After an open system has taken in and utilized external energy and matter to sustain and evolve its pattern of organization, it expels and excretes that transformed energy and matter into its external environment as randomized energy and restructured matter that can be utilized as sustenance by other open systems. This dynamic interchange and recycling of energy and matter between an open system and its external environment is a reiteration of the outside-in, inside-out model of the initial creative process. It maintains the vital continuity and homeostatic balance (the health) of that system and its environment. It is the consciousness and creative intelligence of *The One*, innate in every living system that enables each system to exchange resources with its surroundings while concurrently maintaining its unique pattern of identity. This consciousness also enables each system to creatively adapt to ever-changing external conditions or to influence those conditions to adapt to the system's needs.

The dynamic interchange and recycling of energy
and matter between an open system and its external
environment maintains the vital continuity and
homeostatic balance (the health) of that system
and its surroundings.

Without openness and a self-sustaining dynamic exchange of
matter and energy with the external environment, a living system
will gradually disintegrate into the entropy of non-being. As
Cambridge chemist and researcher Peter Coveney points out:

> For isolated systems that exchange neither
> energy nor matter with their surroundings, the
> entropy continues to grow until it reaches its maxi-
> mum value at what it is called thermodynamic
> equilibrium. This is the final state of the system when
> there is no change in the macroscopic properties—
> density, pressure, and so on—with time.[3]

In other words, an isolated, closed system is ultimately doomed
to a terminal state of non-being in which all identity and future
potentialities for that particular system are lost forever. This terminal state is death by entropy and passive equilibrium. Thus, a
persistently closed system is eventually a dead system with no
hope of rebirth and future possibilities.

As previously discussed, ingesting the outer world, assimilating
its useful resources, and expelling the transformed residual by-
products to the outer world is a phenomenon consistent with both
consciousness and life. This creative act transpires far from the
passive equilibrium of unconscious non-being. In fact, the healthier and more vital a system is, the farther from passive,
thermodynamic equilibrium it dwells.[4] In other words, the more
actively and consciously a living system engages life and creatively
participates in life's continual transformation, the healthier and

more vital that system is. For such a system to continually transform, however, it must continually risk itself in the face of chaos. Let us express this idea in a more personal way.

> The healthier and more dynamically vital a system is, the more creative it is and the farther it dwells from the entropic state of passive equilibrium.

The more actively, consciously, and openly you engage life and participate in its adventure, the more vital and healthy you will be. The courage to engage life with the fullness and passion of your whole being and to risk yourself so that you may find yourself appears to be a prerequisite for growth, creativity, and learning. It requires a willingness of the egoic self to be vulnerable to the transforming chisel of life's artistic hand. When you live life in this manner, you live courageously and passionately with authenticity, and all those who are influenced and touched by your example will be made richer and more alive. You are a character in life's continuing drama as it is played out for the purpose of developing new and more complex structures and behavior that allow for continued growth, evolution, and adaptation. To play your part well, you must creatively, actively and honestly engage the outside world. Such engagement is only possible though, while living in the realm of maximal creativity far from the passive stagnation of a life lived in fear and denial.[5]

Let us ponder this idea for a moment, as it may be relevant to each of our lives. How much would we learn, grow and develop and how much would the world around us benefit if we remained intellectually and emotionally closed; were unwilling to interact on a "give and take" basis with our surroundings (friends, family, coworkers, community); and were reluctant to risk change, denying ourselves the enrichment of new and varied experiences? How independent and productive is the *grossly* autistic child who is locked within his/her own mind-world, unable to relate freely with the rest of humanity? How healthy, viable, and disease-resistant are the offspring of a gene pool whose diversity has been circumscribed by many generations of restricted inbreeding? How resilient is a relationship, a marriage, a family, or a community that lacks respectful, but open and continuous sharing of insights, viewpoints, and subjective experiences among all persons involved? Finally, how healthy is an individual whose neurotic fears and cognitively distorted ideas ignite antisocial behavior at the slightest hint that the chaotic real world may disturb his/her fastidiously ordered personal environment? The answer to these questions should be quite obvious.

Death by entropy vs. death by transformation

There are two kinds of death a living system can experience: *death by entropy* and/or *death by transformation*. Death by entropy and passive equilibrium is demise into non-being. By this death, all evidence of the primary pattern of organization (the core identity of the system) is completely dissolved into maximal entropy where there is no exchange of energy, no order, and no future potentialities. This disintegration is what happens to the physically embodied or *material* pattern of organization of a living system when its animating consciousness (mind) or life-sustaining energy (vital force) is removed. This is the death a physical body eventually undergoes after the consciousness and vital force of the individual self which it embodied are no longer capable of sustaining that self's identifying pattern of organization in material form. From this death, no new, more complex pattern of order arises out of the preexistent material pattern, and the arrow of time no longer points to the future of evolving creativity and continuous creation for that form. In fact, from this death, even the arrow of time vaporizes into nothingness.

As the creation and continued manifestation of life is associated with The Three Hidden Splendors, death by entropy occurs for three reasons dictated by those same three creative principles. These reasons are as follows:

1) *Deficiency of Power:* The system's energy to maintain its pattern of organization, its vital force, is insufficient and unable to sustain:

   a) The core pattern of organization on any level of manifestation;

   b) The core pattern of organization in the realm of maximal creativity, on the edge of chaos;

   c) Continuous evolving creation by being able to transport the system from one state of order, through temporary chaos, into a new state of higher order and greater complexity.

2) *Deficiency of Mind:* The system's consciousness is unable to facilitate and direct the continuous organizing process that in-forms and en-forms the system of its pattern of organization because:

   a) It has insufficient strength or is no longer focussed or fully present within the system.

   b) It no longer holds or manifests a clear concept of the system's individual self-identity and purpose.

3) *Deficiency of Substance:* The system's elements that embody the system's pattern of organization are no longer able to maintain the system's structure because:

   a) They are unresponsive to the influences of that system's consciousness and/or energy.

   b) They are deficient, inadequate or absent.

The *transformational death* by chaos, on the other hand, is a *death into resurrection.* It is death that occurs due to the dynamic restructuring of a system's pattern of organization out of which a new, more complex type of order emerges. Additionally, this death occurs only in far-from-equilibrium conditions "away from the repetitive and the universal to the specific and the unique."[6] Under such conditions, the consciousness of a living system becomes more acute and sensitive to external stimuli. As Prigogine describes it, "In equilibrium matter is 'blind,' but in far-from-equilibrium conditions it begins to be able to perceive, to 'take into account,' in its way of functioning, differences in the external world."[7] In this way, the consciousness of the system becomes more aware of itself and its external environment. This enhanced awareness allows the system greater creative flexibility to adapt. When it is then plunged into temporary chaos its old pattern destabilizes and it more easily evolves and adapts by self-reorganizing to a higher, more complex and novel order of functioning.

Self-organization on the edge of chaos

Self-organization, according to Capra, "has emerged as perhaps the central concept in the systems (or wholistic) view of life."[8] It may be the evidence of life's creativity and consciousness. It occurs in all living systems. It is observed in fluid dynamics, the behavior of chemical systems, the formation of weather systems and traffic patterns, the growth of cities, and the evolution of stars. It is dependent upon iteration and feedback loops and spontaneously occurs (autocatalyzes) in open systems that maintain themselves far from passive equilibrium.[9]

Self-organization occurs in all living systems
and may be the evidence of life's innate
creativity and consciousness.

Self-organization is dependent on the formation of interconnected systems called networks. Networks infer information exchange and cooperation. They are, therefore, dependent upon open communication and cooperation among the parts and the whole to maintain their interconnectedness. They are dependant on their relationships with each other.

Cooperation is a consequence of the mutually respectful nature of beneficial intra-system relationships. In living systems, cooperation is paramount to self-organization and the dynamic equilibrium of homeostasis. It exists when all the parts of the system function harmoniously within the "Janus-like" contextual duality of their identities as *holons* (both individualized wholes as well as parts of a larger entity) obeying the will or "prime directive" of the system as a whole.

Cooperation is essential for self-organization and maintenance of the dynamic equilibrium of homeostasis.

We propose that the prime directive of a system is determined by the identity pattern of the consciousness animating that system. The conscious identity defines the system's purpose or *raison d'etre,* which, in turn, determines its physical pattern of organization.[10]

A system's ability to self-organize, self-regulate, and adapt by engaging its external environment is powered by that system's vital force. The vital force also determines the degree to which a system resists entropic degeneration. The greater a system's vital force, the more vigorously that system resists entropy and the farther it dwells from passive equilibrium, functioning nearer to the edge of chaos in the realm of maximal creativity. On the other hand, the weaker a system's vital force, the closer that system comes to the unconscious stagnation of non-being and the entropic death by passive degeneration.

The greater a system's vital force, the more vigorously that system resists entropy and the farther it dwells from passive equilibrium, functioning within the realm of maximal creativity.

Evidence suggests that growth and evolution spontaneously occur within an open, self-regulating, and self-organizing system as that system moves farther away from entropy and maintains its pattern of order closer to the edge of chaos.[11] The reason for this is that a living system must *periodically* enter into the chaos of reorganization to grow and evolve. As it approaches chaos, the system eventually reaches a point of critical instability. At that point, it experiences the *death of transformation* as it enters chaos and its existing order is plunged into transient disorder. Then, spontaneously, the system self-reorganizes and emerges from chaos to be "born again" into a new state of higher order and greater complexity. In this way, chaos assures ever-evolving creativity and enriching transformation. It is the proverbial "Path of Salvation" all life experiences.

Temporary, periodic exposure to chaos assures ever-evolving creativity and enriching transformation.

The death of transformation through chaos is the recurring theme throughout the cosmogonic cycle of life as we discussed in the previous chapter. In the case of the first transformational death of wholeness, greater individualized identity results as consciousness is projected into the illusory world of duality and separation. In the case of the second transformational death where duality and separateness are realized as illusions, the egoic self is sacrificed for the contextual identity of wholeness:

> And when such a realization of the non-duality of heaven and earth—even of non-being and being—will have been attained and assimilated, life—joy will pour from all things, as from an inexhaustible cup. Ego sacrificed, it is given back, and the waters of deathlessness are released to be carried in all directions.[12]

Growth and evolution

Growth and evolution are two of the most salient properties of life. They allow for continuous creation to take place. They are contingent upon the presence of life's circular, organizational pattern (feedback loops and hypercycles), enabling self-regulation and self-organization. We believe the processes of growth and evolution are the result of life's inherent impulse to express itself in order to establish and affirm its "identity."

Through growth and evolution, life defies entropy—being defies non-being—and evolves into states of greater complexity and diversity, assuring ever-expanding possibilities for relationship, self-reflection, and self-awareness. However, *change is intrinsic to growth, and periodic chaos is intrinsic to change.* Consequently, living systems must undergo periodic chaos in order to grow and adapt as they continuously struggle against the unremitting influence of entropy (non-being).[13] As renowned physicist Erwin Schrodinger has written:

> At every step, on every day of our life, as it were, something of the shape that we possessed until then has to change, to be overcome, to be deleted and replaced by something new. The resistance of our primitive will is the psychical correlate of the resistance of the existing shape to the transforming chisel. For we ourselves are chisel and statue, conquerors and conquered at the same time—it is a true continued "self-conquering."[14]

Chaos, like death, is an inescapable reality of life. It is found everywhere in nature as life struggles to survive and self-evolve. Chaos is the root of life's creativity, the cauldron of life's complexity, the crucible for life's diversity, the fabric of life's liberty, the reason for life's unpredictability, and the essence of life's beauty. It is an inherent phenomenon of change and is experienced by all dynamical living systems. It generates new manifestations of complexity and diversity from tiny stimuli. As living systems evolve, the effects of minute stimuli can be rapidly amplified via circular feedback mechanisms to produce periodic instabilities (chaos), resulting in dramatic and profound outcomes that include more intricate levels of order.[15]

> Chaos is the root of life's creativity, the cauldron of life's complexity, the crucible for life's diversity, the fabric of life's liberty, the reason for life's unpredictability, and the essence of life's beauty.

According to evolutionary biologist Stuart Kauffman, living systems exist in the boundary regions near the edge of chaos because there they are guaranteed greater opportunity to periodically engage chaos and greater flexibility to adapt rapidly and more successfully.[16] This assures them maximal creativity and every opportunity to grow and evolve into greater richness and variety, generating configurations that are always new. According to Capra, the ability to generate configurations that are constantly new is creativity and "is a key property of all living systems." He further adds, "A special form of this creativity is the generation of diversity..."[17]

Living systems dwell in the boundary regions near the edge of chaos in the realm of maximal creativity where they have greater flexibility to adapt rapidly and more successfully.

It is well known that the more biologically diverse (rich in various species) an ecosystem is, the healthier and more vibrant and resilient it is. Diversity, as "a special form of creativity," appears to be another prime directive of life because it assures the maximal unfolding of all the possibilities of identity and relationship. Most importantly, however, it also assures a greater unfolding of consciousness because consciousness "expands" in the zone of evolution where there is greater diversity, creativity and novelty—where there is "new experience." As Schrodinger informs us:

> Consciousness is a phenomenon in the zone of evolution. This world lights up to itself only where or only inasmuch as it develops, procreates new forms. Places of stagnancy slip from consciousness; they may only appear in their interplay with places of evolution.[18]

Schrodinger's statement is quite similar to Prigogine's statement, quoted earlier. In that statement Prigogine refers to a system's ability, in far-from-equilibrium conditions, to "perceive, to 'take into account,' in its way of functioning, differences in the external world."[19] In other words, a living system appears to become more conscious and self-aware the farther it dwells from entropic, passive equilibrium conditions and the closer it comes to the zone of evolution where there is the greatest creativity. Isn't it interesting that the "zone of greatest creativity" appears to also be the zone of greatest consciousness and self-awareness? Creativity and consciousness appear to be synonymous or, one might say, *creativity insinuates consciousness.*

Diversity is a special form of creativity.
It assures maximal unfolding of all the
possibilities of identity and relationship and,
therefore, the greater unfolding of consciousness.

The closer living systems are to entropy, the less creative they are; the less creative they are, the more they succumb to mundane, unconscious, repetitive behavior, stagnation, and demise. In the heart of entropy and passive equilibrium lies the ever-present threat of non-being and its associated terrors. Beingness resists non-being; hence, life resists passive degeneration. Because of the self-affirming nature of life, dynamic living systems move away from passive stagnation toward greater creativity, richness, variety, and complexity—toward ever-expanding affirmations of their beingness. But this direction is also the direction toward chaos because living systems cannot creatively evolve without moving through some form of temporary chaos during each stage of development.

Dying to live and the paradox of transcending self

All change must involve some degree of temporary chaos because for anything to change, it must leave one state of order to enter a new and different state of order. Something must be lost for something to be gained; something must die in order for something else to be born into new life. Let's take your living room, for example. Suppose you wanted to redecorate it (change its present state of order). You contact an interior decorator who comes to your home and helps you decide on new furniture, artwork, color scheme, and other details of decor. In a few days, work begins. The old furniture is moved out, drop cloths are put down, and painting begins, with workers in the room all day, paint and supplies scattered everywhere. Obviously, this is a messy scene of chaotic disorder. Eventually the painting is finished and the new furniture is installed. The room's new look is beautiful. There is more elegant furniture than you had before and a more complex and satisfying color scheme. Out of the chaos of redecorating came the new décor of more elegant order. However, for this to have occurred, the old order of décor (furniture, decorations, color scheme, etc.) had to be eliminated. The old order died via change so that the new order could be born. Would it be possible to achieve comparable results without the experience of temporary chaos? Unless you are a magician, you would not be able to manifest a beautiful new living room without transitory disorder and the death or loss of the old order. All change, from one state of order to a new more complex state of order, must pass through chaos.

> All change, from one state of order to a new
> more complex state of order,
> must pass through chaos.

This movement from order through chaos to a new more complex or "higher" order is the process of continual transformation, self-transcendence, evolution, and growth. It is the way and the truth of life. Ironically, because of the ambiguity of life, it is also the process of death. Without the destabilizing, destructive, disintegrating activity associated with death, there would be no transformation, no birth, no new life; theologically, there would be no resurrection without the crucifixion. "In every creative process of life, a destructive trend is implied; in every integrating process of life, a disintegrating trend."[20] Many traditional healing systems have referred to this destructive or disintegrating trend as the "healing crisis." Mystics have termed it "baptism by fire." The mystery of "sacrifice" lies hidden within it. It is a recurrent theme in nature (e.g., the metamorphosis of the caterpillar into the butterfly, the procession of the seasons, etc). In mythology, the phoenix rises from the ashes as death leads to rebirth, and the hero's journey follows a path that leads to self-realization through a self-sacrificial act. Remember though: the transforming effect of death through chaos only occurs in an open living system that maintains itself in the realm of maximal creativity far from the entropy of passive equilibrium, and one that has sufficient vitality to endure the rigors and stresses of chaotic self-transformation.

An intriguing question is now probably arising in the mind of the reader: "Where along the continuum between stagnation and chaos do I maintain myself? Do I live in the realm of maximal creativity far from equilibrium, embracing opportunities for creative expression, new relationships, and enriching experiences as they come my way—learning, growing, and transforming? Or am I immovably planted somewhere near passive equilibrium, caught in limiting, self-imposed routines, anxious and fearful of anything that threatens my brittle microcosm with new, challenging experiences?"

Living on the edge of chaos in the realm of maximal creativity means embracing and manifesting your full potential and identity. It requires of you "the courage to be;" the courage to recognize, appreciate and express your unique pattern and manner of being as an individual and as a part of the whole of life itself. It also requires of you an exercise of personal will that emulates the Divine Will that directed the creation of the physical universe and encourages its continual evolvement.

To live in the realm of maximal creativity and endure the rigors and stresses of continuous transformation and growth, you must, in the words of Paul Tillich, "affirm your own being in spite of those elements of your existence which conflict with your essential self-affirmation." Such conflicting elements can appear in many guises: Feelings of personal inadequacy; temptations that distract you away from your life purpose; and exterior forces that threaten you with ostracism, pain, destruction, and non-being. Fear of these sufferings may cause you to cower from your life purpose and draw back from the edge of chaos toward the stagnation of entropy. Living your ordered pattern of identity courageously on the edge of chaos allows you to live creatively and passionately in harmony with the flow of life itself—growing, transforming and continually renewing. This is living in a fashion consistent with health and wellness.

On the other hand, when you constantly dwell in fearful complacency, close to passive equilibrium, you confine yourself to a narrow domain of monotonously predictable, static order (as opposed to a broad domain of evolving dynamic order), devoid of richness, stimulating challenge, and renewal. This bland setting engenders within its inhabitants ennui, haunting disquietude, and nagging desperation born of the unwillingness to engage and transcend the fear and anxiety of non-being. When you fail to master fear, your power of will is eroded, neutralized and subverted. If you lack the required dogged determination that unceasingly drives one through the resistance of challenging experiences into the beingness of self-actualization, the essence of your being will be poisoned and devitalized by the resultant existential disquietude arising from such a paucity of self-affirming will. The resulting state of such spiritual debility acts as a rich fertilizer for the "morbid soil" of inherited and environmentally-influenced disease propensity out of which illness arises. The irony, however, is that you can not hide indefinitely from life's self-affirming imperative. Its driving urge to be all that it can be will inexorably assert itself despite all of your conscious resistance. If you meet life's invitation to transforming growth with denial, resistance and opposition, its demand for your full participation may unexpectedly declare itself at any moment in the form of devastating traumatic events. These events will most likely propel you into sudden disruptive and painful experiences, presenting no immediately apparent and comforting reason for their manifestation. They are meant to shatter the static crystallizations of life's vital force, caused by prolonged stagnation from fear, and allow that vital energy to flow again so it may revitalize your life with new passion and commitment.

Transformational change, new order, greater life and self-affirmation are realized through the growth and evolution of life. However, hidden in the core of the process of growth is degeneration; within order, chaos; within life, the inevitability of death. One pole of a dyad establishes the polar termini of an experiential continuum. One member of a dyad cannot exist without the other, as the experience of light cannot exist without darkness. Growth and degeneration, order and chaos, life and death, health and disease; these polar dyads essentially express the same experiential continuum. They are all merely illusionary aspects of the one process of continual unfolding, of continuous creation. As we are immersed in the illusory world of duality and maximal contrast, we experience only their dichotomy and opposition and fail to perceive their oneness.

Illness is an aspect of life that serves life by acting as its destructive, disintegrating, and profanizing process. Yet, it is absolutely crucial to health, as death is absolutely indispensable to life. As Tillich writes, "The concept of health cannot be defined without relation to its opposite—disease.... In reality, health is not health without the essential possibility and existential reality of disease."[21] Life is not life without the essential possibility and existential reality of death.

Health cannot exist without disease, and healing is impossible without traversing the chaotic struggle of illness. Thus, healing involves a risk, a sacrifice or loss of something, a death of some kind. It demands great courage and willpower on your part because you must be willing to risk life in order to win life. As Tillich again informs us, "Life must risk itself in order to win itself, but in the risking it may lose itself. A life which does not risk disease—even in the highest forms of the life of the spirit—is a poor life."[22] This willingness to risk yourself for greater life is the key that opens the door to the wellspring of creativity inside of you and the ever increasing richness and renewal inherent in the creative process.

All healing involves a death of some kind.

Creativity is "the elixir of life" that heals and transforms life. Through the creative process you enter that "sacred place," that "zone of evolution" where "the world lights up to itself" as you light up to the world. It is here, in that "holiest of holy" places that you are reunited with the waters of the wellspring of creativity, The Source of the "River of Life" from which all creative energy and vitality issue forth to be manifested as new life. Through every creative act, life fulfills itself. Through every creative act, you transcend the mortality of your separate ego-self of *I* and enter the realm of immortality to become one with your contextual self as *Thou*, as a self-realized collaborator in creation. Through creativity, you are delivered from the chaos of illness into the dynamic order of new life.

Illness is the physical evidence of life risking itself to win itself. It is the very process through which one must pass to experience one's healing.

The transition from life through death to new life is the Hero's journey and it is a creative process. It is the journey of life's continuous creation. As the characters in life's story, we are all assured of this journey if we are willing to periodically risk ourselves and surrender the illusory security of our comfort zones to engage the possibility of egoic death by living more passionately, openly, and creatively as *The One*. By consciously engaging the possibility of egoic death, we are assured life. By consciously engaging the possibility of illness, we are assured healing.

> We have only to follow the thread of the hero-path. And where we had thought to find an abomination, we shall find a god; where we had thought to slay another, we shall slay ourselves; where we had thought to travel outward, we shall come to the center of our own existence; where we had thought to be alone, we shall be with all the world.[23]

A word of caution

Lest we be misunderstood, admonitions for reason and caution are appropriate here. Dwelling on the edge of chaos as a key to self-realization does not mean engaging in the reckless and fool-hardy pursuits of unbridled egoism. Activities that threaten life and limb in frantic pursuit of the next momentary thrill, the next "adrenaline rush," are common distractions that some people use, like brain-altering substances and mindless entertainment, to escape the haunting desperation within their own hearts by focusing the ego-mind on tantalizing exterior matters. There are those who would rather face wild beasts in the arena, armed combat on the battlefield, or the physical agony of a daredevil feat gone awry than to sit quietly in solitude and engage honestly the shadows lurking beneath the surface of their own egoic personalities (their fear, avarice, bigotry, selfishness, hatred, xenophobia, pettiness, and other aspects of their "shadow" self). For many people, these specters within are too terrifying to face and are consciously acknowledged as aspects of their own selves, so they are projected outward onto other people, groups, ideas, things. Nevertheless, healing transformation cannot take place without recognition of these shadows of the egoic self and their loving confrontation and exposure to the light of truth. Only this can purge their pathologic influence from one's consciousness.

Second summary of living systems

- All living systems are holons and exist as both part and whole. They simultaneously display separate and contextual identity.
- All living systems grow, adapt, self-replicate and evolve into greater, more complex and integrated wholes.
  1) Each new whole preserves and embodies the characteristics of its separate parts while negating their separateness and adding a more complex and grander identity.

- All living systems embody some degree of consciousness and creative intelligence exemplified by:
  1) Their unique pattern of organization;
  2) Their ability to self-organize and self-regulate in response to stimuli from their external environment;
  3) Their ability to grow, adapt, self-replicate and evolve.

- The extent to which a living system embodies consciousness and creative intelligence is directly associated with the extent to which it:
  1) Resists entropy;
  2) Creatively responds to its external environment;
  3) Undergoes continual change, and embodies "newness" as exemplified by its ability to grow, adapt, and evolve.

- The dynamic vitality or "health" of a living system is determined by how well that system:
  1) Maintains its unique pattern of organization far from

equilibrium on the edge of chaos;

2) Responds to its external environment;

3) Creatively adapts to its external environment or influences its external environment to adapt to its needs;

4) Maintains its individual and contextual identity as both part and whole.

Chapter 9

The Victory of Death and the Hero's Journey

*"When our day has come for the victory of death,
death closes in; there is nothing we can do,
except be crucified —and resurrected;
dismembered totally, and then reborn."*

Joseph Campbell, from *The Hero With A Thousand Faces*

*"When a society calls for a new hero to arise,
it also calls forth the conflict from
which that hero is to be born."*

Patrick Donovan, Mystery School,
Bastyr University, Winter 2003

Born to die

The "thread of the hero's path" inevitably leads to death, but not the final death of entropy and non-being. It leads instead to the transforming death of resurrection through which the hero's life is transfigured into new life. This death is only made possible, however, by a sacrificial act. The hero must ultimately sacrifice his ego-illusion of separateness for the realization of his contextual identity—his "oneness" with all life. Thus, the multi-faceted identity of *The One* that lies within him can be continually realized and celebrated into new life.

Few can better describe the hero's journey and its link to the cosmogonic cycle of life than Joseph Campbell, when he writes:

> The cosmogonic cycle is presented with astonishing consistency in the sacred writings of all continents, and it gives to the adventure of the hero a new and interesting turn; for now it appears that the perilous journey was a labor not of attainment but of re-attainment, not discovery but rediscovery. The godly powers sought and dangerously won are revealed to have been within the heart of the hero all the time. He is 'the King's son' who has come to know who he is and therewith has entered into the exercise of his proper power—'God's son' [as consciousness] who has learned to know how much that title means. From this point of view the hero is symbolical of that divine creative and redemptive image which is hidden within us all, only waiting to be known and rendered into life.[1]

Dying from one realm of existence in the cycle of life is tantamount to being born into another realm, another level of consciousness or organizational complexity. Every birth demands a death of some kind as every hero demands a conflict of some kind. Life in physical form derives much of its meaning and preciousness from its struggle against entropy and the fact of its fragility and mortality. For life to continually grow and evolve it must continually change, continually die. As Paul states in I Corinthians 15:31, "I die daily."[2] Old patterns must die for new ones to be born and established. One must "die daily" to be reborn daily. In life, death is inevitable because change is inevitable.

Every birth demands a death of some kind as every hero demands a conflict of some kind.

Continual change is the seed process hidden within the womb of every archetypal pattern in nature. Without change, there is no growth, adaptation, or creativity—there is no life, because life is the *process* of continuous change. As Roman Emperor and Stoic philosopher Marcus Aurelius instructed:

> Unceasingly contemplate the generation of all things through change, and accustom thyself to the thought that the nature of the universe delights above all in changing the things that exist and making new ones of the same pattern. For everything that exists is the seed of that which shall come from it.[3]

Lexicographers define "process" as "a systematic series of actions or changes proceeding from one to the next" directed to some end or goal; the action of continuous change; a moving forward as part of a progression or development. As one ponders these definitions, it becomes clear that *life is process.* It is a verb, not a noun. It is dynamically active and continually changing, growing and developing. As process, it is not a material *thing* that can be touched, tasted, held in the hand or physically quantified. Material things are the evidence, results or artifacts of process, frozen like snapshots of moments in the time-continuum of conscious experience. Process is the underlying truth of matter; the particle is only the *localized illusion,* the "shadow" of process "witnessed" into manifestation by individualized consciousness. Life can only be experienced as an internal, subjective reality of the self in response to the sensations and perceptions created by a continual series of external stimuli. What we humans sense as matter, the things of the physical universe, are merely crystallizations of consciousness (thoughts, beliefs, concepts); the "props" with which consciousness plays out its self-revealing and self-transcending psychodrama as life. As William Shakespeare has written, "All the world's a stage, and all the men and women merely players: they have their exits and entrances, and one man in his time plays many parts."[4]

Life, as process, can only be experienced as an internal, subjective reality of the self in response to the sensations and perceptions created by a continual series of external stimuli.

Life is a systematic series of births and deaths proceeding from one to the next. What is it that must die so that new life can arise? The elements of existence that conflict with life's essential self-affirmation must die. They must be sacrificed because they are the factors that constantly pull life back toward the constrictive, entropic abyss of stagnant changelessness and non-being, away from the edge of chaos and the "zone of evolution."

Living on the edge of chaos, in the realm of the hero, forces you to be ever vigilant for opportunities to "nullify the unremitting recurrences of death" by continually being reborn. As Joseph Campbell reminds us, "Only birth can conquer death," so there must be "... a continuous 'recurrence of birth' *(palingenesia)* to nullify the unremitting recurrences of death."[5] The hero conquers death by being reborn out of chaos into a new, more creative and self-actualized being.

As open, living systems, each of us must be continually reborn, minute-by-minute, day-by-day. But to achieve this, we must continually discard, as a sacrificial act, that which is no longer life-generating and life-affirming. Old patterns must die to make way for the new. This continual dissipation and elimination of energy and matter is what Campbell refers to as "the unremitting recurrences of death" that must occur to allow the "continuous recurrence of birth." As an ancient Asian saying goes, "If one wants to drink fresh tea, one must be willing to empty one's cup of the old tea."

Since a viable living system must be in the continual process of exchanging energy and matter with its environment, something within the system must be continually lost (die) so that something else can be continually gained (born). This principle underlies the theological and mythological significance of *sacrifice* as well as the significance of *catharsis* in psychology and *cleansing elimination* in healing. This transformational process of dynamic turnover and replenishment assures the continuity and vigor of life.

Something must be continually lost
so that something else can be continually gained.

Transformation through sacrifice and surrender

The hero's odyssey is the pilgrimage through death to greater life. It is the journey from the unconscious to the self-conscious, from non-being to self-realized being. Although it initially entails the affirmation of self as *I* (as ego), the hero's journey is ultimately fulfilled through the affirmation and transcendent recognition of self as Thou; as the contextual self, standing in continual evolving relationship *with The One, as The One.*

When you realize this truth you affirm your self-transcendent identity as *The One* and "you become through your relationship to the Thou" and "as you become *I*, you say *Thou.*" *(See Chapter One)* However, this experience requires that the primary word—*Thou*—be spoken, felt and lived with the whole of your being. As Buber tells us, "The primary word can only be spoken with the whole being. He who gives himself to it may withhold nothing of himself."[7] The giving of your self in this way is an act of total surrender. It is an act of unconditional love. You are "set free" through this act; free from the anxiety, fear, and loneliness of living in the illusion of duality and separateness.

This act of surrender is the second "death," the turning point in the spiraling, recursive cosmogonic cycle of creation. It is the point where *The Many* again become *The One*, where "God beholds God," and the *I* of separateness becomes the *Thou* of wholeness and integration. It is here where the mystic and the hero renounce the dualistic illusion of the material realm in order to, as Campbell writes, "…retreat from the desperations of the wasteland to the peace of the everlasting realm that is within."[8] In Buddhist and Taoist traditions this is called "turning the light around" and is used as a technique for clarifying the mind.[9] In fact, all true spiritual practice is designed to turn the gaze of the ego-mind (the Janus-faced self) away from the mesmerizing distractions of the outer illusory world of "subordinate parts" and material things toward the inner, real world of integrated wholeness where The Source of all things dwells and the wellspring of creative process lies. From this place, the hero, as the symbol of self-aware consciousness, is restored to wholeness as he surrenders his individual ego-self to *The One* while sacrificing his dualistic illusions of separateness. In this place, the hero is reaffirmed as *The One* while *The One* is self-realized as the hero. Each fulfills the other as each reflects the other.

Self-reflection reveals the hero to himself as the embodiment of life. Upon seeing and *knowing himself* as such, "the efflorescence of the light" that is within him "increases in magnitude" and he undergoes a stunning metamorphosis from *I* into *Thou*.[10] The inscription "Know Thyself" was emblazoned above the entrance to the ancient Greek Temple of Apollo at Delphi, for this reason. This may be what is meant by the statement, "God lies within."

In the sacred space at the core of your own being you enter into relationship with your greater or contextual-self. From this relationship the seed of God-essence is germinated and the god within is born as you affirm yourself as life through the death that leads to greater life—the death of the illusory separate self as ego alone. As Tillich tells us, "Self-affirmation is the affirmation of life and of the death which belongs to life."[11] Here lies the true mystical meaning of sacrifice and of healing. As Jesus teaches us in Mathew 11:39, "He that findeth his life shall lose it: And he that loseth his life for my sake shall find it."[12]

This sacrificial, transformational death rarely occurs all at once. It is a phenomenon that occurs in a systematic series of changes proceeding from one to the next on various levels and in diverse aspects of your life as you slowly realize your contextual identity and surrender, little by little, through compassion and love, to the process of transformation. As you sacrifice your ego-self, out of love, to embrace someone or something greater or more precious than that of egoic self, your greater, contextual self is realized. In this sense, *I* is lovingly and nobly sacrificed for *Thou*.

To sacrifice is to offer, give up or surrender something prized or desirable for the sake of something considered as having a higher or more pressing claim. The surrendering of the egoic illusion of separateness to the integrated *wholeness* of *The One* is the hero's gift. But it is not an easy gift to relinquish. Most of us are dragged into the experience by the seat of our pants, kicking and screaming. Bit by bit, however, we slowly acquiesce under the summons of life's self-affirming mandate to undertake the hero's journey and its ultimate sacrifice. Surrendering turns us away from egocentric living as an isolated *I,* alone in its illusion of separateness.

The sacrifice of ego-surrender also entails the relinquishing of old beliefs and thought patterns rooted in fear engendered by the false, anxiety-ridden attitude of "me against the world." Most importantly, the existential fear of non-being, death, and oblivion is relinquished as are the relentless feelings of guilt, self-condemnation, and meaninglessness.[13] To what are they surrendered? They are surrendered to the purifying flames of chaos to be re-forged by the process of continuous creation into new life. As John Briggs and David Peat state:

> In each moment, we have the opportunity to die psychologically by letting go of prejudices, mechanical habits, isolation, precious ego, images of self and world, and conceptions of the past and future. In this way, we set in motion the possibility of a creative, self-organizing perception that puts us in touch with the magic that gave us birth.[14]

Following the hero's path

The hero's path is the transformational process of life. Following that path is a profoundly intense process that often feels agonizingly unbearable. Following it successfully depends on your ability to:

• Have faith in the regenerative process of life and in your essential value and worthiness in the grand scheme of things.

• "Keep your eyes on the prize" and "keep hope alive" by consciously and consistently focusing your vision upon your image of a positive, fulfilling, and productive future at a new level of order and creativity.

• Develop and sustain a sense of connectedness to all living things and a purpose and personal meaning in your life by involving yourself in creative endeavors that will serve life in some way.

• Feel in control of your life by realizing your freedom to make effective choices.

• Maintain an attitude of enthusiasm, joy, and inspiration by consciously savoring, on a moment-to-moment basis, the sensual deliciousness of life's experiences and its exquisite beauty.

- Feel deeply a sense of personal destiny, as part of a greater plan.

- Sustain a sense of humor that helps avoid taking too seriously the challenges of daily living and the ego's response to them.

- Maintain a "burning desire" to fulfill your path of destiny through the hero's journey.

It is interesting to note that these are not unlike the characteristics identified by researchers as indicative of persons with strong adaptation skills, for whom stress does not seem to increase susceptibility to disease. Such persons are termed "hardy" individuals.[15] The characteristics of the "hardy" person are also the characteristics of the hero. The "hardiness" of these individuals, which evidently protects them from adverse, pathological reactions to the stresses of exposure to chaos, is, in fact, their *flexibility* (the ability to self-reorganize and adapt creatively to the inevitable constancy of change).[16]

Persons lacking "hardiness," on the other hand, are more susceptible to the entropic death by rigid stagnation and resistance to change. They succumb to diseases of suppressed identity and denied self-realization. According to researchers in the field of psycho-neuro-immunology, some of the characteristics of persons lacking "hardiness" are:

- Rigid, inflexible attitudes and beliefs.
- Resistance to change.
- Poor coping and adaptive skills.
- Weak psychological defenses.
- Feelings of hopelessness and helplessness.

- Poor self-esteem.
- Unwillingness to acknowledge and authentically express emotions, particularly negative ones, in a healthy way.[17]

For you to remain connected to the whole of life is of invaluable assistance along your journey. You should, like the holon you are, be ever cognizant of your individual and contextual identity simultaneously. In this material realm of the relative, your relationships are the prime-directives that reinforce life's essential unity and meaning. Many of the tribulations of life's chaotic events can be avoided or attenuated by the loving emotional support of your family, friends, and colleagues. According to researchers Barbra Dorian and Paul Garfinkle, for people experiencing the stress of change, "empirical studies have confirmed that exposure to stressors by individuals receiving adequate support does not increase the risk of mental and physical illness. The mechanism by which social support is thought to be protective involves facilitation of coping and active mastery."[18] Remember: A healthy living system must maintain a vigorously dynamic network of open, beneficial interactions between its parts and the outside world (the whole) in order to be self-sustaining and evolving. The health of any living system depends upon the quality of the relationship it maintains with its environment.

The health of any living system depends upon the quality of the relationship it maintains with its environment.

The hero's journey of self-affirmation proceeds at a variable pace, with progress occurring daily to various degrees in all aspects of your life. It may require a new way of interacting with your spouse, child, coworker or friend. It may demand facing the challenge of personal loss, divorce, disease, or other traumatic events. If you have the courage to affirm your true nature, to choose to dwell in the realm of maximal creativity on the edge of chaos, to embrace inevitable change as it arises, and to release your ego's fearful illusion of isolation and separateness, you will complete your journey victoriously. This is a noble mission of high purpose to which you can be wholeheartedly dedicated. It is the path congruent with Divine purpose and truly worthy of a self-realizing child of the Creator.

Do the best you can each day. Every personal interaction, every opportunity for choice offers a platform to affirm who you are and who you choose to be in that moment. Every self-affirming choice that encompasses your contextual relationship to the whole moves you farther along the hero's path. Be aware, even the greatest heroes periodically stumble or falter under the yoke of responsibilities, personal demons, and character traits that need to be healed. Yet, even this faltering is a blessing in disguise, because it offers the opportunity to discern, through *non-judgmental* introspection, precisely where your healing intention needs to be focused and your transformation needs to take place by surrender and sacrifice.

There are no right or wrong choices on this path of continuous creation. There are simply choices and the consequences of those choices. Therefore, it would be prudent to choose responsibly, considering the long-term consequences to your life and to the lives of others. (Decision-making among many Native American traditions historically involved considering the consequences for the next seven generations.) At the same time, however, be prepared for outcomes you could not anticipate. These are frequently unexpected opportunities that merely require additional choices. If you are mired in value judgments of right or wrong (within your accepted bounds of ethics and morality), you may fall prey to the self-defeating practice of judgment and self-criticism that inevitably leads to guilt, the hidden nemesis of self-affirmation.

As we stated earlier, if you are not willing to risk the current state of your life in order to embrace a greater state of beingness, the ever-advancing procession of life will continue in spite of you. It will assert itself through disease and/or physical demise if it is constantly met with rigid resistance, inflexibility, and suppression. Death is inevitable, as is change. When it knocks at your door in the guise of chaotic turmoil, no matter how minor or grand, you will not be able to avoid it. Yet, you are free to choose the kind of death you will experience—transformation or stagnation—and the kind of consequences you will have to face. Will you choose a transformational death, traversing temporary chaos to be reborn to greater life? Or will you choose the death of persistent denial and defiant resistance to change, riddled with the self-inflicted suffering of fear, regret, guilt, and blame? The latter is the death of cowardice that does not dare to risk itself, while the former is the death of the courageous self, willing to risk itself in order to find itself.[19]

Chapter 10

Illness and the Healing Journey

*"For its operation, the body of a living person
has two immaterial entities to thank —precisely
those to which we generally refer as consciousness
(soul) and life (spirit). It is consciousness which
presents us with the messages that are manifested
in the body and eventually made visible as disease."*

Thorwald Dethlefsen and Rudiger Dahlke,
from *The Healing Power of Illness*

Caught in the confusion of chaos

There is an inherent danger within every transformational process. Illness and dysfunction can arise from the temporary instabilities that occur in a living system's dynamic pattern of order (its identity) as that system periodically transitions through chaos while moving along its path of continuous creation. These transitional periods of instability are dangerous because at such times, a living system becomes vulnerable and fragile. For us human beings, the temporary instabilities we experience from the stresses of various chaotic life events can disrupt and confuse us to the extent that we lose sight of our purpose and direction in life no matter how hard we struggle to "stay the course." This especially occurs when we unconsciously resist the inevitable changes of life's dynamic process. It also occurs if the realization of our contextual identity and/or its affirmation and expression are obstructed or derailed by the vicissitudes of life's traumas.

Various aspects of a living system's identity or pattern of organization become momentarily disordered on some level as that system encounters stimuli that produce instability. This causes the system to slip into temporary chaos. If the system lacks either a sufficient intrinsic vitality enough to carry it through this transient instability, or a clear conceptualization of its new pattern of order, disorder becomes prolonged. Prolonged disorder causes the system to then become mired in chaos and unable to complete the transition to the next level of complexity and order. If it is unable to maintain the old order as well, the system will most likely become dysfunctional. Its boundaries distinguishing self and nonself will become distorted and ambiguous, and self-identity will be called into question. *Illness arises from this dysfunctional state of confusional paralysis.*

The extent to which a living system manifests illness when caught in this state of dysfunction is directly related to:

1) The initial *vitality* of the system;
2) The characteristics of the *triggering stimuli;*
3) The *intensity of chaos* into which the system has been plunged;
4) The *magnitude of resulting disorder* it undergoes;
5) And the *degree of resistance* it generates to transformative change.

There is an irony here, however. As we discussed in previous chapters, the disorder of chaos from which illness arises is an integral aspect of the process of life—changing, growing and continually creating. Thus, illness is an integral part of life's continual transformation as is chaos. As such, illness can not be eliminated, "cut out," poisoned into oblivion, resisted or ignored out of existence. It can only be used as a vehicle to transform life into greater life. As Thorwald Dethlefsen and Ruduger Dahlke write: "Our purpose is not to resist illness but to use it... [because] healing arises exclusively from the transmutation of illness never from conquering symptoms."[1] (There are, however, definite occasions when "conquering" or "palliating" the symptoms helps one transmute the illness.) Through this transmutation, the illness itself becomes the healing path, the mystical or mythological "elixir" or "potion of life" that, when ingested, brings eternal life.[2]

Illness is the destructive trend implied in every self-sustaining process of a living organism. It is the balancing, disintegrative counterpart to every integrating process. Without the potential for illness and disease, life could not proceed on its path of continuous creation because continuous creation is dependent upon continuous destruction. Life, in the physical sense, is what it is only within the context of the reality of physical death. Health exists as an existential phenomenon only in juxtaposition to the phenomenon of disease. Therefore, the time-honored motto of healing—*Vis Medicatrix Naturae* ("The Healing Power of Nature")—is only a half-truth. Within this concept lies its "shadow side," the full, paradoxical, hidden truth of the destructive power of Nature. Without a full understanding of this living dialectic in its wholeness, we are left with only a partial truth. As we have discussed in Chapter Two, the universe exists in its wholeness because of the paradox of duality and maximal contrast. Life cannot be denied its death as light cannot be denied its darkness.

Consider the forest floor. It is strewn with the residue of death: the rotting wood of dead trees; the decaying plant matter; the putrefying carcasses of dead animals and insects. To most people caught in the judgmental space of the ego mind, this rot and decay is disgustingly repugnant and something to be avoided. But bacterium, fungi, worms, and flies and other insects feed on this rotting material. Eventually the decaying material, as well as the organisms feeding upon it, is degraded to simple, stable substances (water, nitrates, urates, ammonia, minerals, and carbon dioxide) that diffuse into the soil. These substances then nourish new life. The process of demise, rot and decay, perceived as "disgusting" and fearfully avoided as the remnant of disease and death, when understood in the context of the forest as a whole, is the very process that sustains and nurtures the vitality of all life in the forest. It is an essential and vital aspect to the fertility, health and well being of the forest. Similarly, the dreaded experience of illness provides the means by which Tillich's "elements of your existence [ego-generated illusions] which conflict with your essential self-affirmation" are degraded and broken down into the pure substance of your true essence of being to be used to nurture and feed your healing transformation, self-affirmation and, eventually, your self-transcendance.

The experience of illness is the very process by which healing is achieved. It is the process through which one's essential self-affirmation struggles to assert itself against the stagnation of non-being. But the truth of this can only be realized if the natural process behind it is understood and accepted in its *full* meaning and context. Unfortunately, most of us in today's "modern," Western culture have been denied the full truth of life—denied its shadow side, by the various socio-religious influences that have shaped our culture. As a result, the majority of us are overly preoccupied with avoiding and denying all expression of "the shadow" and its truth of illness and reality of death, instead of learning how to courageously engage it and allow it to teach us the way to our healing transformation. As Dethlefsen and Dahlke state, "Illness is not some accidental, and therefore disagreeable upset along the way, but the very way itself along which people can progress towards wholeness."[3] There is an old mystical saying: "Where the fear is, there you go." In other words, one must go into and through the darkness to get to the light.

Within the illusion of duality, illness and health are polar opposites along the same linear continuum of life and continuous creation *(See Fig. 10-1)*. A true continuum extends infinitely in both directions and can be infinitely divided in a way similar to a fractal. Thus, it is difficult to pinpoint where, along the continuum, illness begins and health ends. It is all relative to where you are on the continuum at any given time. One place on the continuum at one moment may be on the side tending toward illness. As you move down the continuum, that place that was fostering disease is tending now toward health. When you regard the continuum with a wholistic perspective, however, preconceived demarcations distinguishing health and disease become ambiguous. Health and disease are then seen as two aspects of the same process—the process of continual creation. As physicist Fritjof Capra suggests, echoing thousands of years of mystical thought, "There are, in truth, no distinct opposites, no absolute experiences belonging to different categories." There are only "two sides of the same reality; extreme parts of a single whole."[4]

The Continuum of Life and Continuous Creation

Health	Illness
Dynamic Order (Integration)	Disintegration
Wholeness	Fragmentation
Dynamic Balance (Homeostasis)	Chaotic Imbalance
Birth	Death
World of Light (day)	Shadow World (night)
Spring & Summer	Fall & Winter
Generation & Nurturing	Degeneration & Decay

Fig. 10-1: The Continuum of Life and Continuous Creation

Consider also this example. If you walked into your boss' office at work, knowing he had a history of health problems, and found him breathing rapidly and heavily, coughing with every few breaths, his pulse bounding and racing, his face flushed and perspiring, laying back in his chair as though he were in great distress, you would probably call "911." These are clear signs of disease. Or are they? What if he had just returned from a ten-mile run? The symptoms he was experiencing would not be symptoms of illness at all. Ignorant of the full context of your observation, you interpreted your boss's appearance as illness when, in reality, he was merely displaying signs of a relatively healthy person becoming healthier. What appears as disease may be, in reality, the evidence of health *when the full context* of the situation is realized in its totality. What is perceived and experienced as health or disease depends on where you are on the continuum of life. Often, what you consider to be illness at one moment might only be the manifestation of life adapting, evolving, and reorganizing to a new level of order and complexity. You may just be experiencing it in a temporary, transitional phase as it passes through chaos along its cycle of continuous creation. In a different moment along the timeline of continuous creation, you may look back and see it as such and be thankful for its outcome. Many cancer patients over the years have told us how thankful they were for their cancer saying: "It was a blessing that changed my life."

Defining health and illness

Based on the multidisciplinary perspectives we have presented, we would like to redefine and clarify conceptions of health and disease. We use as fundamental principles the First and Second Summaries of Living Systems as presented at the end of Chapters Six and Eight respectively. We recommend reviewing these ideas and fully contemplating their wide-ranging implications before considering the following definitions.

Health

Health is the functional result of a living system's full engagement and participation in the process of continuous creation while simultaneously maintaining its individual and contextual consciousness as *The One.*

Illness

Illness is the consequence of a living system's resistance to the process of continuous creation while adhering to the illusion of separateness, unconscious of and/or resistant to its contextual consciousness as *The One.*

When your individualized ego-mind refuses to submit to the contextual awareness of continuous creation, you resist the transformational mandate of life itself. You deny yourself the death that masks the hidden victory of the eternal life within. As it is written in John 12:25, "He that loveth his life shall lose it; and he that hateth his life in this world [the world of duality, separateness and isolation] shall keep it unto life eternal."[5] When you deny yourself healing transition through chaos, you condemn yourself to passive, stagnant, entropic demise as the potential for realizing your true identity gradually dissipates.

Illness at its core

Illness occurs when a system's consciousness (Mind) fails to realize its contextual identity and/or is unable to facilitate and direct the transformation of its unique pattern of organization toward continuous creation. The consequences of such a shortcoming are:

- The *elements* (Substance) that embody the system's pattern of organization are no longer able to maintain that system's structure. We believe this failure establishes a predilection toward such diseases as chronic autoimmune disorders (e.g., rheumatoid arthritis, lupus, multiple sclerosis, etc.) and degenerative disorders (e.g., osteoporosis, accelerated aging, Alzheimer's disease, and cancer).

• The *energy* (Power) or "vital force" of the system dissipates, becoming insufficient to maintain the pattern of organization. We believe this collapse allows the emergence of such diseases as chronic fatigue syndrome, emotional apathy and depression, anorexia, anxiety disorders, cachexia (wasting), and AIDS.

More simply stated: illness often occurs when you fail to risk death for new life. Healing and the continuity of life require a death or sacrifice on some level. The death ultimately involves the ego and the sacrifice is always associated with the ego-illusion of separateness and Tillich's "elements of existence" that resist your essential affirmation of being. Resistance to your essential affirmation of life and being requires a great deal of effort and energy expenditure. More often than not that resistance is eventually worn down by life's persistent self-affirming imperative. At that point, the sacrifice is eventually made in spite of you and death is eventually risked for new life.

Sometimes this "death" leads to the demise of the physical body. Over the more than forty years of patient care experience between Dr. Joiner-Bey and myself, we have often seen patients die healed. In such cases, the physical dying process is the vehicle for the spiritual healing needed by the consciousness of those patients in order to free them and transform them. Remember: Consciousness is primary and is so much greater than the physical structure it utilizes for its brief sojourn through time on the physical plane.

According to theological and mystical traditions, if an individual constantly resists life's invitation to be continuously creative on the highest level of consciousness ("the spirit"), death by passive stagnation will eventually set in. Relentless resistance to life's self-affirming imperative ultimately causes the disintegration of the absolute identity of that individual into the nothingness of non-being.[6] We suggest this is the meaning of the second death referred to in Revelation 20:14. This is the death of absolute identity (death of entropy) into the oblivion of non-being, to the extent that one's identity or "name" is no longer "found written in the book of life."[7] It is caused by the relentless refusal of an individual to participate wholeheartedly in life's continuous creation as a unique individualized, yet integral part of the whole—of *The One*.

Know thyself

The challenge of chaos can destabilize your life and shatter your belief systems to the core. It can weaken and erode the boundaries distinguishing self from non-self causing identity confusion to occur. The greater the challenge of chaos, the more unclear your boundaries become and the more self-identity is called into question. This obscuring and eventual disintegration of identifying boundaries catalyzes the beginning of self-reorganization and transformation, forcing you to thoroughly reassess your life and personal path. This is the time when it is most crucial to "retreat from the deprivation of the waste land" of separateness and isolation of the *I* "to the peace of the everlasting realm" of wholeness and contextual identity of the *Thou* that lies within. Here you will be reunited with the truth of who you are as an integral part of the whole— as *The One*. From this "sacred place" you can chose and act appropriately, because from here the view of your purpose in life and path of transformation is made clear. Without this clarity of identity and purpose, you may get caught in a continuous cycle of chaos out of which illness can arise.

Illness can arise in the absence of a conscious realization or an instinctive sense of:

- Who you are in *contextual relationship* as The One,
- Your *purpose* and personal *meaning* in life,
- Your *personal desti*ny or purpose as part of a greater plan.

Without an anchoring self-knowledge of who you are at the deepest level of contextuality (your connection to *The One;* to The Divine), you may become lost within chaos as your superficial and illusory perceptions of self degenerate under chaos' disruptive, yet transforming stress. Realization of any new pattern of self-reorganization, in this case, will be obstructed and transformation through chaos into new order will not occur. Your contextual self-knowledge is your umbilical cord to your Source—to *The One;* your lifeline through the chaos to the new, more complex order of the transformational process. Lacking some general sense of your contextual identity and the direction and purpose of the transformation hidden in the chaos confronting you, you may find yourself lost in the disorder of illness with your freedom to make the best contextual choices greatly circumscribed. Unwise choices can cause further resistance to transformational changes and lead to more chronic disorientation, confusion, and disorder. And so, the cycle of chronic disease is established as entrapment in this quagmire of perpetual chaos continues and propagates causing self-identity to become grossly distorted, lost or confused.

Think of the endless disruption that would ensue if you were planning to remodel your house but your contractor started tearing down walls before you had any plans drawn up for him to follow or had crystallized a new concept for the interior and exterior design. Without a clear conception of the new design for your home and well-conceived blueprints to guide the remodeling work once it had begun, your house would be subjected to continual chaos and might even be destroyed!

When you have no conscious realization or instinctive sense of your true contextual identity, purpose, or destiny, when your identity is not "rooted" in the wholeness of *Thou,* individual self-identity can disintegrate into disquieting ambiguity when faced with various chaotic life events. When this occurs, the boundaries defining *self* dissolve into confusion; the "morbid soil" of disease, composed of the interacting influences of genetics, diet, lifestyle, the environment, and other toxic factors becomes seeded and impregnated with a disordered pattern of consciousness. With no ordered, cohesive identity pattern of consciousness to modify and buffer the morbid influences of disease, illness takes root at various levels and to varying degrees within mind and body. You would be surprised to know how many patients with chronic diseases have no idea or vision of what their life would be or look like if they were healed.

The consciousness of disease

Traumatic life events can disrupt personal boundaries and wreak havoc on any conscious realization or instinctive sense of contextual identity, purpose or destiny a person might have. To survive these events, the human psyche often has to suppress, *for a period of time,* the associated feelings and thoughts generated by the trauma. However, once the immediate event is over and that person has "survived" the initial trauma, the associated thoughts and feelings are commonly too frightening to revisit. Those thoughts and feelings and the message of transformation they carry with them, are then all too often ignored into chronic suppression. But they must be experienced and their message must be heard, so they push back against the suppressive energy. The resultant internal conflict and fatiguing, energetic demands are like "dry rot" to a person's consciousness, and they provide food for the "dragons" of fear hidden deep within the shadow world of the unconscious.

When you fail to resolve the psychological and emotional issues that arise from life's traumatic events and suppress them from healthy expression over many years, their disruptive, energetic influence can induce abnormal biochemical, neuro-endocrinological and cellular responses that result in illness. The intensity and character of their pathologic influence on cellular function depends upon the status of the morbid soil or *disease propensity* within your physical and psychological constitution and the strength and clarity of consciousness and self-identity forming and shaping that constitution. Familial, genetic, dietary, environmental, and lifestyle factors determine the "fertility" of the soil for disease expression. Protracted disintegration of your personal and contextual identity and your sense of purpose in life by the dry rot of internal conflict from suppression and denial can drown consciousness in identity confusion at a fundamental level. Bathed in the spatial field of your identity consciousness, your cells and tissues (the *substance* of your physical identity) will reflect that confusion. Further, taking their sense of identity from the confused organism, they will manifest this ambiguity as structural disorganization and functional disregulation. If the constitutional "soil" is morbid enough and the disruptive external influences are traumatic enough, illness is inevitable.

The issues are in the tissues!

Individual consciousness, greatly conditioned and programmed by familial, cultural, and global consciousness, has a greatly underappreciated influence on disease manifestation and pattern of expression. It can function as a catalyzing pathologic agent in receptive constitutional soil. Consciousness may determine the pattern of disease expression in the physical body as it informs and enforms matter. Cellular events and physiologic changes can mimic identity crises occurring at a higher psycho-emotional or spiritual level. For instance, one can become "inflamed" with anger, "heart-broken" with grief or "blind with rage." Though some may argue that these are merely metaphors, these descriptive relationships exist in other languages. Some have suggested this reflects a universal subconscious, metaphorical relationship between the psycho-emotional issues and certain pathological phenomena.

Functioning as interacting aspects of a whole being, they are not segregated phenomena. Mind and body are one. Both are simply varying manifestations of consciousness. The physical body is consciousness solidified. Consciousness is the informing and enforming reality. Any ambiguity of conscious identity nebulizes the pattern of organization of the living system. (Remember: Mind acts on substance through power to inform and enform that substance into physical form.) As Dethlefsen and Dahlke write, "Illness is a human condition that indicates that the patient is no longer in order or in harmony at the level of consciousness."[8]

> Cellular events and physiologic changes can mimic identity crises occurring at a higher psycho-emotional and spiritual level.

This concept of mind-body link, and its influence on health and disease, is not new to human thought. For millennia, it has been a quintessential aspect of the belief systems and healing prac-

tices of diverse cultures from simple indigenous peoples to complex civilizations. Over the past twenty years, with the advent of
psycho-neuro-immunology (PNI), modern scientists have discov-
ered some of the rudimentary properties of the mind-body
relationship and its channels of communication. Mounting experimental evidence elucidates its clinical significance.[9] Through
complex interactions among the central nervous system,
endocrine system, and immune systems, thoughts and emotions
(conscious and unconscious) have immense impact on physical
well-being and overall state of health.[10]

It is now understood in modern neuro-biochemistry that every
emotional state that a human being experiences has an associated
pattern of neuropeptide production within the central nervous
system that is released into the bloodstream for dissemination
throughout the body. More than fifty of these compounds have
been identified. Receptors for these chemicals have been found on
cell membranes of tissues in many organ systems. Thus, these neu-
ropeptides have biochemical influence on the functioning of
many different kinds of cells. Consequently, every emotional state
you experience has almost ubiquitous functional impact on your
tissues and organs. Mind and body are inextricably linked.[11]

Association between certain personality types and specific diseases has been recognized within many of the ancient empirical
healing systems—traditional Chinese medicine, Ayurvedic medicine of India, and classical homeopathy. Until a few years ago
there was little documented scientific evidence to substantiate
such associations. However, recent studies have corroborated to
varying degrees the observations and conclusions made by those
empirical practitioners.[12]

Preliminary studies by Stanwyck and Anson of Georgia State
University in the mid-1980s, correlated specific clusters of illness
presentation to specific personality patterns. Using data from the

Minnesota Multiphasic Personality Inventory (MMPI), a respected tool for determining personality types and pathologies, they were able to identify five cluster groups with the most distinctive personality profiles consistently associated with clinically diagnosable physical illness. These five cluster groups were the foundation upon which the now-accepted Five Factor Model of Personality was developed.[13]

Cluster Group 1
- Rarely occurring in "normal" people
- Most frequent profile types among psychiatric patients
- Characteristic presentations:
  - Depression
  - Indecision
  - Hopelessness
  - Severe low-esteem
  - Chronic fatigue
  - Physical weakness
- Associated physical disorders:
  - Alcoholism and eating disorders

Cluster Group 2
- The "sick" cluster
- Convert readily psychological stresses into physical disorders
- Identify problems as external instead of internal
- Tend to deny psychological involvement and personal responsibility
- Associated with a number of illnesses
  - Heart disease
  - Asthma
  - Arthritis
  - General medical disorders
  - Multiple sclerosis
  - Headaches
  - Cancer

Cluster Group 3

- Tend to be angry, moody, unpredictable, non-conforming, and emotionally shallow
- Experience problems in social communication and thinking
- Associated with addiction and rheumatic heart disease

Cluster Group 4

- Identical to Group 2 except the psychological characteristics are much more pronounced
- Associated with:
  - Multiple sclerosis
  - Intestinal disorders
  - Non-organic back pain
  - Pain in general

Cluster Group 5

- Essentially "normal" with no outstanding associations with disease

Other personality factors have also been linked to increased susceptibility to autoimmune diseases, particularly rheumatoid arthritis. According to Doctor G. Solomon, female patients with rheumatoid arthritis are more likely to "show masochism, self-sacrifice, denial of hostility, compliance-subservience, depression, and sensitivity to anger than their healthy sisters and are described as always having been nervous, tense, worried, highly strung, moody individuals."[14]

With regards to autoimmune disorders, such as rheumatoid arthritis, in which one's immune system attacks one's own tissues (self attacking self), it is not surprising to see masochism, self-sacrifice, denial and suppression of hostility, compliance-subservience, depression, and sensitivity to anger as underlying influences. The mindset of autoimmunity is a consciousness of "me against myself" in which one becomes one's own worst enemy and critic. The suppression of rage and the frustration of unrealized, unaffirmed identity caused by disintegrating, confused self-identifying boundaries can turn the emotional charge inward against oneself. Conscious and subconscious imprinting of this pattern of self-critical masochism and denied hostility upon one's tissues infuses the morbid constitutional soil with the precise blend of biochemical and energetic influences that conform the inflammatory and degenerative tissue changes associated with autoimmune disorders to one's "inflamed" attitude towards oneself.

There is also the classic Type A personality, originally described by cardiologists Meyer Friedman, M.D. and Ray Rosenman, M.D., in the Journal of the American Medical Association (JAMA) in 1959. Until the early 1980s, it was thought that this personality type, described as aggressive, competitive, and overachieving with a strong sense of time urgency, was at increased risk for coronary heart disease, stroke, and untimely death. However, according to more recent research at Duke University Medical Center, in the late 1980s by Redford B. Williams, M.D., Professor of Psychiatry, "It's not talking fast, feeling pressed for time, and putting in long hours that will kill you. It's being suspicious of and hostile toward your fellow humans that will do you in."[15] It appears that of all the psycho-behavioral attributes ascribed to the Type A personality, only those grounded in resentment, fear, anger, and the hostile, extreme patriarchal-dominant attitude of "me against the world" increase the risk for heart attack, a disease outcome historically more common in males. Dr. Williams says that this heart attack-prone, hostile personality is comprised of three aspects: "cynical mistrust of other people's motives (such as believing that most people will lie to get ahead), frequent feelings of anger, and aggressive expression of hostility toward others without regard for their feelings."[16] The mindset of this type of personality is clearly associated with the illusion of separateness and the fear, mistrust, suspicion, and hostility engendered by isolation.

The self factor

Even on the biological level, the question of identity plays a very important role. There is a very special way in which the consciousness of the mind and the pattern of organization and function of the body are closely linked. They both contain the ability to sense and recognize identity as self vs. non-self. Through this characteristic capacity of consciousness to distinguish self from non-self, the mind and body are able to perform the most basic function vital to resisting disease and preserving self. At this most rudimentary level, establishing and realizing identity is crucial.

Within the human body, the duty of distinguishing self and non-self is the responsibility of a particular subset of white blood cells (WBCs) in the immune system called the T-lymphocytes.[17] All living cells have "recognition molecules" or "molecular identification badges" on their cell walls or membranes. This phenomenon of nature allows WBCs to distinguish indigenous cells of self from foreign invaders. The capacity to discriminate is developed in infancy and is the basis for the survival of complex organisms in environments teeming with potential microbial pathogens threatening entropic disintegration. This same ability by WBCs is paramount to identifying and eliminating indigenous cells that have become malignant rogues, threatening the survival of the entire organism by abandoning their mutually respectful and supportive roles relative to other cells.

Self is the composite identity of an organism on all levels of experience and expression—physical, emotional, intellectual, and spiritual. It provides the template by which personality and consciousness are shaped, adaptation skills are developed, and the reactive mode by which the challenges of life and stresses of chaos are experienced and managed. Any threat to self on one level is invariably perceived as a threat to self on all levels, because the mind and body are bidirectionally linked. All threats to self present the self with chaos and the potential for non-being.

The characteristics and boundaries that define self or personal identity are relatively stable and easily recognized on the physical level. They include the morphological traits of the organism enclosed in skin or other exterior membrane, shell, etc. The boundaries that define self and personal identity on the level of consciousness (psycho-emotional-spiritual levels), however, are more subtle and difficult to define. They are intangible, mutable, ethereal, abstract, contracting and expanding, and ultimately capable of encompassing all time, space, substance, and personality.

When personal identity, as self, functions within the physical body in a healthy way, that which has been identified as self is not perceived as a threat, while that which is considered non-self is perceived as threatening. Confusion of self-identity, ego dissatisfaction with self (self-criticism, self-hatred, poor self-esteem, internalized oppression, etc.) or phobic mistrust of the external world, can poison the healthy functioning of self-discernment and blur and obscure the boundaries of self causing:

- Identity at the cellular level to go awry, resulting in cell *de-differentiation* from committed, differentiated cell types (nerve, muscle, skin, etc.) back to primordial forms free of their specific differentiated identity; back to a place again where they had choice. These undifferentiated forms commonly proliferate indiscriminately as cancerous lesions outside the boundaries of cellular contextual identity.

- *Hypersensitivity* (allergies) to harmless aspects of the external environment perceived as threatening thereby stimulating the development of allergic disorders, such as asthma and environmental hypersensitivities.

- The self to be inappropriately perceived as a threat resulting in the *autoimmune phenomenon* of self immunologically attacking self, chronic inflammation, and degenerative disorders such as lupus, rheumatoid arthritis, multiple sclerosis, Crohn's disease, Hashimoto's thyroiditis and Grave's disease.

For all living organisms, the normal response to a threat entails five primary actions:

1. *Recognition* (distinguishing self from non-self);
2. *Stimulation* (increased activity of all systems relevant to protection of self);
3. *Neutralization* (confrontation/interaction with the perceived threat leading to avoidance, destruction, or transformation of the threat through cooperation, adaptation and symbiosis);
4. *Elimination* (removal of the threat and any related issues or neutralization remnants);
5. *Resolution* (self-reorganization and return to homeostasis).

When this response is confrontational (me against you, myself, the world) a great deal of energy is expended. The outcome of this kind of interaction is dependent on the strength of self ("hardiness") relative to the strength of the threat. If at any time the threat is stronger than the self, the process of neutralization may become prolonged. This pathologic power relationship can prevent complete elimination and resolution, causing either destruction of self or ensnarement of the self in the confusion and disorder of protracted chaos and chronic disease.

Depending on its nature, a threat, perceived by a healthy, hardy, secure self, may not be interpreted as a danger to self but as an opportunity for growth. In this light, symbiosis, adaptation, and transformation can occur. The threat is transformed adaptively and incorporated into self, and cooperation occurs rather than confrontation. Self then expands into new levels of order, creativity, and wholeness. This is how living systems evolve and avoid extinction.

Cooperation appears to be the key to the survival of living organisms and is based on the hierarchal model of actualization. Many "weak organisms" have survived by forming collectives "while the so-called strong ones, never learning the trick of cooperation, have been dumped onto the scrap heap of evolutionary extinction."[18] According to microbiologists Lynn Margulis and Dorion Sagan, "Symbiosis —the living together in intimate association of different kinds of organisms—is more than an occasional odyssey. It is a basic mechanism of evolutionary change."[19]

The disordered identity of cancer

We believe consciousness determines the pattern of organization or structure of the physical organism—the body. Therefore, ambiguity and confusion of self-identity may be associated with derangement at the cellular level. An excellent example of disordered identity at the cellular level is cancer. It is truly a disease of deranged identity at the very core of cellular life. DNA, the most fundamental biological control of the expression of cellular identity, goes awry, failing to sustain the specific functional identity of the cell.

All cells in the human body arise from a single fertilized egg. Daughter cells of the fertilized egg replicate and progress through primordial, undifferentiated cell types. As they become more specialized, they first form the embryo and then the fetus. To produce a complex living entity comprised of numerous, *harmoniously interacting* organ systems, the cells must develop ever-increasing specialization. Skin, nerve, liver, blood—these are merely a few examples of familiar cell types into which primordial daughter cells must differentiate. Under the influence of nuclear chromosomal DNA and the contextual relationship with other cells, almost every cell in the body maintains its identity and serves a specific functional purpose that harmoniously supports the well being of the whole organism and every other cell therein. Establishing the cell's structural and functional relationship to the whole organism via differentiation and specialization of form and function (the enforming of the cellular substance) creates the hallmarks of identity at the cellular level.

Cancer manifests at the cellular level when the biological phenomena that maintain cells in their differentiated, specialized state of individual and contextual identity become dysfunctional. When this occurs, cells lose their sense of relationship to the whole—their contextual identity—and become de-differentiated or de-specialized and proliferate excessively without harmonious regard for neighboring cells or the whole organism. The regression of a cancerous cell back to a more primordial state is reminiscent of the uninhibited individual freedom of a single cell life form and the undifferentiated state human cells have before they are committed to differentiating into specific types of tissue cells. In this regressed state, the cell is free to choose a new path of self-identity and self-expression because it is free of the identity imposed upon it by its relationship to the "whole." No longer contextualized by the extracellular matrix and controlling biochemical agents of the body, the cell abandons its relational identity for the illusion of separateness, and it no longer behaves as an integral part of a multi-cellular life form. This rebellious cell is driven to survive as singular and separate, at the cost of the whole, in a posture of "me against the world" or, in this case, "me against the body." From a different point of reference, the cancer cell becomes an *I*, refusing to recognize the *Thou*. Uncoupled from *Thou*, the cell no longer responds to the controls of internal and external relationships that define identity.

The extracellular matrix (the environment within which the cell exists) plays a major role in the cell's differentiation and contextual identity, as does the family, community and social environment within which we live with regards to our own personal identity. According to cell biologist Mina J. Bissell, "It is now a universal concept that the microenvironment outside cells, of which an important component is the extracellular matrix, confers tissue specificity."[20] Unresponsive to its external environment (its contextual identity), the aberrant cancer cell then terminates its membership in and its productive contributions to the whole community of cells and excessively proliferates to ensure its own, individual immortality.[21]

The cancer cell is no longer able to respond to the internal and external control systems of contextual identity:

- Tumor suppressor genes are turned off;
- Proto-oncogenes are turned on,
- Cell-cycle clock goes awry and the natural cyclic rhythms are ignored;
- Cell-to-cell communication is ignored;
- Fail-safe systems fail.[22]

As the cancerous cells proliferate and tumors are formed, excessive demands are made on surrounding tissues and the organism to support the unbridled perpetuation of the cancer cell line. Because these cells share no mutually beneficial relationship with the whole, there is no reciprocation by the malignant cells. They take all and give nothing of value that sustains surrounding tissues. This is a parasitic relationship of conquest and subjugation, rather than integration and cooperation. This relationship exhibits attributes of the extreme patriarchal domination model as discussed in chapter three and is exemplified by "corporatism" and the environmentally-insensitive corporate conquest of the Earth's eco-system. This relationship is diametrically opposite to the feminine activation model of partnership and cooperation *(See Chapter Three).*

As the malignancy proceeds, it is oblivious to all morphological boundaries and ruthlessly invades and conquers the surrounding tissues through infiltration. Destroying the structural integrity of surrounding tissues, the tumor cells plunder all nutritional resources in an act of "cellular terrorism" not unlike the "global terrorism" we are presently facing. Metastasis establishes colonies of these ruthless, egocentric, terrorist cells throughout the organism. Cachexia (muscle wasting and malnutrition), resulting from nutritional depletion, develops as resources are sapped. The community of normal cells begins to die. Cellular necrosis (cell death) and the demise of the whole organism are the ultimate outcome.

The Seven Stages of Cancer:

Cellular de-differentiation
Proliferation
Infiltration
Metastasis
Cachexia
Cellular necrosis
Death

Cancer, in our opinion, is exemplary of a disease process in which one's sense of identity has gone awry. It biologically depicts the illusion of separateness and the consciousness of "me *against* the world" or "me *alone* in the world," in stark contrast to context, harmonious relationship, and selflessness. The consciousness suggestive of cancer is a consciousness afraid of or resistant to the death of the ego-self, refusing or unable to sacrifice the egoic illusion of separateness in order to manifest true contextual identity.

This can best be illustrated by the patients we have seen diagnosed with cancer whose life stories have revealed histories of unrealized self-expression and identity crises. Due to familial and sociocultural constraints or unresolved psycho-emotional traumas, they have been unwilling or, more often, unable to realize fully and live passionately their true personal identity in relationship to the world. The suppressive survival mechanisms that initially helped them survive life's traumas have become the very "elements that resist" and obstruct their true self-affirmation of being on some level. Unable or unwilling to risk losing the familiarity and security of these antiquated survival mechanisms, they are ironically forced into facing their own mortality by having to make life and death decisions relative to their potentially terminal diagnosis. They are forced to face their shadow and the truth of life's transformational death despite the resisting will of their ego.

There is another aspect of the consciousness of cancer we have observed in some of our patients in the course of our clinical work.[23] It is one of egocentricity. The patients who maintain this consciousness often seek unconsciously to *satisfy only their own needs* either by passive-aggressive behavior that avoids direct confrontation, or by assertively deluging persons in their environs with diatribes of self-serving justifications for forwarding their own existence at the expense of all those around them. This presentation is more an outgrowth of the consciousness that epitomizes the "me against the world" mentality of separateness and isolation as opposed to "me alone in the world." Such a person must die to the illusion of separateness and be reborn to the truth of their contextual identity with the rest of humanity. The diagnosis of a terminal disease and the ensuing chaos is often exactly what such a person needs to burst their bubble of self-illusions. Healing may come from realizing their own mortality and allowing themselves to have faith in something greater than themselves and to trust and depend on others needed to help them through their disease process. From this humbling experience of faith and needing others, the patient can finally realize his/her relational identity and be able to sacrifice his/her illusion of separateness and isolation for the reality of wholeness.

It is interesting to note the parallels between this cancerous disease process and the state of the modern world and history of civilization based on the attitude of "me against you" and "us versus them." Human affairs have been permeated by malignant belief systems influencing the thought and behavior of people everywhere. It is no wonder why our modern world has been witnessing such a dramatic increase in the occurrence rates of and mortality from cancer. We presently live in a world saturated with malignant (cancer) consciousness.

Most of our patriarchal-dominant institutions (political, religious, educational, military, corporate, economic or medical) commonly act to perpetuate their existence as agencies of wealth and power, regardless of adverse effects on individual free-will choice and various communities, including their own low-level employees and stock-holders. As with cancer cells, these institutions function as separate entities of power with little regard for the contextual reality of their existence except when it directly relates to their immediate profit or gain. Just think of the recent corporate scandals associated with Enron, Adelphia, Worldcom, and others.

The ego-centered, profit-driven, corporate-industrial consciousness is an excellent example of the consciousness of malignancy which is rooted in the domination hierarchal model as discussed in Chapter Three. In its insatiable pursuit of unparalleled power and wealth, the corporate-industrial establishment has contributed mightily to the environmental, social, and cultural upheaval of the planet and indigenous peoples worldwide as it rationalizes its behavior with a plethora of pacifying arguments. Nearly three quarters of all cancers in the world, as well as a number of neurological and immunological illnesses, are linked to its industrial waste and by-products. Where there is the mindset of malignancy, there are also the carcinogenic byproducts of that consciousness. As it has been so wisely stated, "...the tree is known by its fruits."[24]

A weakened, distorted, or unrealized sense of identity; feeling helpless and hopeless; a feeling of unending entanglement in chaos; and resistance to traverse the hero's path make one more susceptible to the ego-dominant world consciousness of malignancy, and contribute immeasurably to one's disease susceptibility. Oftentimes, it is this global influence that imprints a corrupting pattern of disease upon one's consciousness while its carcinogenic waste products poison the physical body. This tendency is especially insidious for the fetus *in utero* and children at high risk due to genetic and lifestyle factors. When these factors are present as a "fertile soil," it may be the world or familial consciousness of malignancy that finally catalyzes the disease process from which childhood cancers and other childhood disorders eventually manifest.

The consciousness of the cancer cell is
"Me against the world!"
Its prime directive is "Survival at all costs!"

The consciousness of the extreme, patriarchal-
dominant, corporate-industrial complex is
"Us against the world!"
Its prime directive is "Survival at all costs!"

Choosing the way of health

We propose it may be possible to positively transform an existing illness or minimize the propensity for disease if the disease pattern has not been so repetitively and deeply imprinted or enformed into the fabric of cellular and tissue structure and function that its resulting pathology is irreversible. This can be done by choosing the hero's path and transforming the disordered consciousness that is informing and enforming the disease process into a consciousness of wholeness.

You must choose the heroic path at every opportunity, embracing transformational change, contextual self-identification, and dynamic relationship with *The One*. The sooner this is done, the better, because the consciousness of the material world is so dense. It took years for your consciousness along with lifestyle and genetic factors to influence your body's current condition both positively and negatively. Thus, it can take years of restorative influence from a new, transformed consciousness and healthy lifestyle to finally transmute the current diseased substance of your body (or of the world) into that of health. A rule of thumb among naturopathic physicians is that it may take a month of committed healing work to reverse the adverse effects of each year of irresponsible, self-destructive lifestyle choices. Of course, this rule is subject to the unique recuperative powers of the individual patient.

Choosing the hero's path means choosing the way of wellness. The work on this path is *transformation*. The process is *surrender*. And the vehicle is *faith*.

Chapter 11

Instruments for Transformation

*"Only love and the lover
can resurrect beyond time.
Give your hearts to this;
the rest is secondhand."*

Jelaluddin Rumi, 13th century Islamic-Sufi poet

The substance of faith

Faith is defined biblically as "the substance of things hoped for and the evidence of things not seen."[1] We prefer to describe faith as *knowing and acting as if one's desired goal has already manifested.* Faith requires a clear, realistic concept and visual image of that which is desired or else it can become "blind faith." This conceptualization or visualization (to the best of one's ability) is critical to its fruition. It is surprising to us how many of our patients want to be healed but have no idea of what that would look like or be like. They actually have no concept of *who* they would be if they were healed (i.e., how would they be living their life on a daily basis? What would that look like down to every detail?). How can you be healed if you have no concept of what that means? How can you get anywhere if you have no idea of where you are going? To be healed you must know and be able to visualize the "new order" into which you are transforming and through faith, live that new order daily as if you were already healed—already whole.

Faith can also be described as the *placing of complete trust and confidence in something more powerful and of greater magnitude than oneself.* As we described earlier in Chapter Two, *process* is what is real while *things* are the illusive shadows of that reality. Therefore, it would be unwise for anyone to place one's faith in material things. It is wiser instead, for one to place one's faith in the eternal, *transformative process* of life's continuous unfoldment. This creative process is the substance of *The One*'s splendor and the evidence of *The One*'s essence and nature gloriously manifesting. It is the only constant in life that is always dependable. You must discover this for yourself and come to know it in your own personal way. Through it you will enter into sacred relationship with all life.

Faith is a passively active phenomenon. It creates a space in consciousness for that which is desired. It allows, rather than commands. It *yields* to the probability of manifestation rather than forces it. Even in the very beginning, according to Genesis, light was brought into existence through an act of faith. God said, "*Let* there be light." God did not say commandingly, "Be light." To *let* is to allow or permit. The term connotes openness, free will, and lack of ego-attachment. God let the light come forth. God didn't "make" it happen. But what was God "letting" bring the light into existence? God was letting the conscious, continuous creativity of God's own nature bring forth the light. The faith was *in the process of God's own nature*—the continuous creativity and eternal unfolding of life through the immutable laws or archetypes of that process.

The eternal unfolding of *The One* is the story of life. It is told in the continuous generation and unfolding of every single life form. Only through faith in that continual, creative process can each one of us surrender to the eternal unfolding of life, and only through surrendering can we be transformed and reborn to complete the hero's journey of divine self-affirmation.

The instruments for navigating the hero's journey are *thinking, imagination and desire*.[3] These are the instruments of creativity. The personal price the hero must pay for passage along the way is *service*. What is it the hero must serve? The hero must *serve life* because the hero *is* life!

Thinking, imagination and desire

Every decision you make, problem you solve, action you take, emotion you feel, and thought you think, no matter how apparently mundane or insignificant, affects you, changes you, and transforms you in some way. It informs and enforms you. Furthermore, because you are a part of the whole, a "holon" in the holographic network of life, your thoughts, feelings, words, and actions affect all those with whom you have ever entered into relationship. As they are affected, so do they, in turn, affect you and the others to whom they relate. This is the "web of life" of which we are each a strand. Ultimately, each one of us affects the *whole* universe. Therefore, who you are and choose to be can change the world. As you are transformed, the world is transformed. As you are "lifted up" in consciousness, the world is lifted up in consciousness. This is a universal theological truth. We are reminded of it in John 12:32 when Jesus states, "And I, if I be lifted up from the earth, will draw all men unto me."[4]

Through your thoughts, feelings, and choices, you are self-reorganizing internally and recreating the world externally in every moment. You are continually dying and being reborn. You can never be exactly the person today that you were yesterday. Some part has died, and some part has been transformed. Science substantiates this fact on a physical level. For example, cells are constantly dying and being replaced. New proteins are being synthesized to reform and replace old tissues. Even bone tissue is being constantly broken down and built up as it is renovated to meet physiologic needs. A living human being is a dynamic *process* rather than a static *thing*. We are integral to life's creative process and are in perpetual creative expression, born of and maintained by life's Three Hidden Splendors. Each of us is molded by a distinct identity pattern of consciousness and empowered by the vital force of individualized will, as it manifests physically through the unique genetic structure of our DNA.

The more willingly you embrace the chaos that confronts you to find the order within and the message it carries for new life, the more opportunity you have for creative transformation and growth. Therefore, as you live your life more consciously, creatively and courageously, you open yourself to a wider diversity of possibilities and choices. In order to choose wisely the best path to your fullest expression and affirmation of being, you need a clear understanding of who you are individually and contextually and a vision of the most fruitful and creative direction for your life. You also need the will to transcend the inevitable vicissitudes of chaotic change in order to "rise from the ashes" of chaos to express your new self-affirmation of being. To do this, you must "retreat from the desperations of the wasteland to the peace of the everlasting realm that is within."[5] The fundamental desperations are those born of the illusion of separateness. The inner peace, in which you find everlasting refuge, resides in your contextual identity, in your harmonious relationship with the whole—with *The One*, as *The One*. Within this eternal reality are the instruments of transformation to guide your course and the consistency of the most sacred relationship: *I/Thou.*

In everyday life, all decisions you make and creative matters you undertake are directed by the Three Hidden Splendors of *Mind, Substance, and Power* experienced as *thinking, imagination,* and *desire,* respectively. As creative principles, they are our instruments for transformation and self-affirmation.

- **Mind as *Thinking:*** The forming and maintaining of a concept or process continually in the mind.

- **Substance as *Imagination:*** Visualizing or creating a mental picture or image in the phase space of mind; the "substance of things hoped for."

- **Power as *Desire:*** Wishing, craving, or longing for with all one's being; the creative impulse of *The One.*

Through introspective thinking and inquiry, you can "retreat to the realm within" to uncover your true "identity" in relationship to *The One.* You can observe and contemplate the boundless diversity and abundance of life around you and rejoice in that life. More practically, you can explore all of the choices and possibilities that have accompanied and continue to accompany the chaos of each new event in your life, and ascertain which of these best fit your evolving sense of being. You must, as the great axiom states, "Know Thyself" and remain attuned to your evolving identity. In other words, recognize your "pattern of organization" and the "structure" of your essential nature. The "pattern" and "structure" are revealed in your talents, interests, and personal and family histories. Delve into those histories. Explore personal, professional, and family relationships. Recall major traumatic events and how you responded to them. Review academic, professional, and creative pursuits. Most importantly, revisit forgotten dreams and aspirations. Know your family of origin. What is their story? How has their story formed and shaped you? These are the rich resources that can help reveal your identity and provide contextual meaning to your life and raw materials for new possibilities.

The compensations and adaptations you have made in your life due to these factors, as well as the consistent patterns of behavior and/or recurring themes, can reveal your direction and purpose, issues to resolve, identity to be transmuted, and identity to be affirmed. The kaleidoscopic array of experiences, choices, consequences, and their effect on your thoughts, feelings, behavior, and self-image constitute a record of your human existence that has sculpted who you are consciously and subconsciously. In other words: know your story!

In all biological systems, identity is revealed by a system's structure, pattern of organization and, most importantly, its story (i.e., the history of structural changes it has undergone resulting from various influences).

In biological systems, identity is determined by:

- Structure
- Pattern of organization
- Process/Memory (The history of physical, emotional, psychological and spiritual changes resulting from various influences)

Once you have explored your story; recognized your evolving identity in relationship to *The One*, as *The One*; and have chosen the direction that promises the greatest opportunity for self-realization, you must again apply the three creative principles reflected in the Three Hidden Splendors. Thinking and imagination mold the universal substance of your creative potential into the form matrix of your new self. Through desire, thinking impregnates the womb of your imagination with your new identity. Desire, in harmony with the action of living that new identity forthrightly in the outer world, sets the pattern of your new identity into vibration and brings it into actualization. Desire is above wanting. Wanting is just the egoic self reaching and grabbing. True desire is the creative impulse of *The One*.

Tilicho Lake

In this high place
it is as simple as this,
        leave everything you know behind.

Step toward the cold surface,
        say the old prayer of rough love
            and open both arms.

Those who come with empty hands
        will stare into the lake astonished,
there, in the cold light
        reflecting pure snow

the true shape of your own face.[2]

– David Whyte

Become a conscious collaborator with *The One* in the creation of your new life. Think it. Desire it. Know it. Speak it. Act it daily in faith. Then, through total surrender of the egoic *I* with its illusory beliefs of what "should be," let it go, relinquish it to the creative forces of life and allow them to transform you while having faith that all will be as it must. This way of being is true visualization, true prayer. It is "praying without ceasing" or "living prayer." When you persistently and faithfully apply these principles in this way with an open mind willing to consider all possibilities that come your way and the burning desire to completely surrender to the *Thou* of The Eternal One, miracles happen!

There is, however, a compensatory price to be paid to life for this miraculous gift from life. This payment is tantamount to a spiritual toll for passage along the hero's path. The toll is a gift to life. The gift is the serving of life through a "great and noble deed"—the "hero's deed." This great deed or gift can be as simple as planting a tree, complimenting a person, volunteering at a homeless shelter or donating money or time to a worthy cause. Or, it can be as involved as wisely and lovingly parenting a child or transforming your work into a life-enhancing profession no matter what that work may be. Whatever the choice, it must be done for the benefit of life to promote creativity, growth, diversity, compassion, cooperation and awareness of contextual reality through relationship and community.

The Self-Affirming Life of the Hero's Path

The work is transformation.
The process is surrender.
The vehicle is faith
and the tools are
imagination,
thinking,
desire.

The
payment
is serving life.

It can be said that the ultimate "great deed" is living your life compassionately in harmony with the reality of wholeness and in continuing relationship with *The One*, as *The One*. In so doing, you inform the world of the essential unity within multiplicity. As Campbell states, "The great deed of the supreme hero is to come to the knowledge of the unity in multiplicity and then to make it known" to the world.[6]

The two —the hero and his ultimate god,
the seeker and the found —are thus understood
as the outside and inside of a single, self-mirrored
mystery, which is identical with the mystery of the
manifest world.[7]

A question of identity sparked the creation of the physical universe. That inquiry continues to drive the eternal cycle of life. Answering it impels the "hero's journey" that affirms life's greatest mystery. Each of us is concurrently a singular answer connected to all the other possible answers to this most fundamental question. Every moment we live, every choice we make formulates the reply. We are life's story being told every day. We are life's affirmation of itself and the face of its own consciousness. Be bold and courageous in your living. Ask the question of identity—"Who am I?"—at every moment and in every new situation. Then, behold the answer as you gaze into the face of your own reflection:

"I AM myself the creation!
I AM Life!"

Acknowledgments

First and foremost I must acknowledge Edna Miriam Lister (1884–1971), founder of the Society of the Universal Living Christ. She was a true mystic who lived and taught as a selfless instrument of The Light. This book was only possible because of her transformational work and the incredibly wise, loving and patient teachers (Ruth Johnson, Judy "Lotus" Landice, Hellen Effinger and Ross Whitehead) who shared with me her work and lived and continue to live the essence of her teachings through the years. I can only hope to live my life in a way that honors them and all they have given me.

Next I must certainly thank Doctor Herb Joiner-Bey. Deep and special thanks to him, not only for his intelligent dialogue and feedback through the many hours of conversations relevant to this book, but also for his years of continued friendship and support. The quality of this book would have been nowhere close to the level it is without his invaluable input.

I thank Janet for her boundless patience and quiet reserve while I struggled, semi-reclused for many hours at a time with this book. Special thanks to David Hiatt who was willing to risk working with this new writer and saw the potential of this book from the very beginning. Special thanks also to Pam Christiansen, artist and patient who underwent and continues to undergo "the journey." Her tremendous insights from her healing, transformative experience can be seen in her three illustrations at the beginning of each section of this book. There are many more to see at her gallery/studio on Bainbridge Island.

I am indebted to a number of friends and colleagues who were gracious enough to read through early drafts and give me insightful and intelligent feedback. They include: Carl Johan Calleman, Ph.D.; Daniel Cicora; Leo Declos; Christy Lee Engles, N.D., LAc.; Nancy Gleiner; Ralph Golan, M.D.; Ben Hines; Monica Liddle, N.D.; Bill Mitchel, N.D.; Mel Morse, M.D.; Ken Ostrander, Ed. D.; Chi Chi and Ron Singler, M.D.; and Leanna Standish, N.D., Ph.D. I am also indebted to John Lapham for his initial guidance and thoughts on cover design. I am especially grateful to Joseph Pizzorno, N.D., my teacher, mentor, colleague and friend, for all he has taught me over the years and for agreeing to write the Forward of this book. A deep and abiding thanks to Z'en ben Shimon Halevi for his kind review and guidance by instructing me to "tell the story," and to Evan Harris Walker, Ph.D., for his astute insights into the nature of consciousness and his thoughtful review of this book.

Finally, unending gratitude and thanks to Janice Phelps for caring, listening and being so kind and gracious as to give me the chance to tell my story and get this book published.

About the Authors

Patrick Donovan, N.D.

Dr. Patrick Donovan is a Naturopathic Physician, author and educator. He writes and lectures on the transformational process of healing. He maintains a busy private practice as a licensed, naturopathic primary care physician at the University Health Clinic in Seattle, Washington and is an adjunct clinical professor at Bastyr University's Natural Health Clinic. His is also the author of *Dancing with The Beloved: Resurrecting Divine Sexuality through Profound Relatedness.* To learn more about Dr. Donovan's work, visit the author's website at www.pdonovan.com.

Herb Joiner-Bey, N.D.

Dr. Herb Joiner-Bey is a seasoned clinician, educator, and author in therapeutic nutrition, botanical medicine, and classical homeopathy. He serves as an adjunct professor, medical consultant, and journal editor in the field of natural medicine. He is the author of four books and dozens of magazine articles. Dr. Bey received a B.A. in Physics from Johns Hopkins University and the degree of Doctor of Naturopathic Medicine from Bastyr University.

Pam Christiansen

The artist for the three pictures at the beginning of each section (and in color on the back cover) is Pam Christiansen. Pam is the founder of The Center For Creative Consciousness on Bainbridge Is., Washington. She has a Fine Arts degree from both California State University and the University of Hawaii and has done graduate work in art history at UCLA. Currently, Pam has been showing her work nationally and has been facilitating workshops for expanding creative consciousness in the U.S. and Canada. A gallery of her work can be seen on her web page: www.pamchristiansen.com

Endnotes

Chapter 1

1. "The transformation of the hero through the dragon fight is a transfiguration, a glorification, indeed an apotheosis, the central feature of which is the birth of a higher mode of personality." (Neumann, E. *The Origins and History of Consciousness.* Princeton: Princeton University Press, 1954, 149.)

2. We would like to clarify the masculinization of this transformational act into the "hero's" deed as opposed to the "heroine's" deed. No prejudice is inferred. The "hero's deed" is an action taken by egoic consciousness. The mythological archetype of egoic consciousness is male while the archetype of the "womb of the unconscious," from which all consciousness is born, is ascribed to the female.(Neumann, E: The Origins and History of Consciousness. Princeton: Princeton University Press, 1954.) Further, the acts of *entering into* a cave and confronting and fighting the serpent of the uroboros to enable the ego to *project itself* into self-realization by freeing itself from the power of the unconscious are archetypically male acts. Entering into and projecting out of are archetypically male acts while being entered into; accepting within, and embracing are archetypically female acts. This is why, according to archetypical thought, males have a penis and females a vagina/womb and the male sperm is selectively embraced into the female oocyte for fertilization.

3. Tillich, P. *The Courage To Be.* New Haven: Yale University Press, 1952, 3.

4. In other words, when the ego "realizes that the support of heaven at the moment of death means nothing less than to be begotten by a god and born anew." (Neumann, E. *The Origins and History of Consciousness,* 255.)

5. Ibid., 255.

6. "The self whose self-affirmation is virtue and courage is the self which surpasses itself." (Tillich, P. *The Courage to Be,* 28–29.)
7. "The fear of death determines the element of anxiety in every fear. Anxiety, if not modified by the fear of an object, anxiety in its nakedness, is always the anxiety of nonbeing." (Ibid., 38)
8. Dethlefsen, T. & Dahlke, R. *The Healing Power of Illness.* Rockport, MA: Element Books, 1991, 11.
9. "The primary word *I-Thou* can be spoken only with the whole being. Concentration and fusion into the whole being can never take place through my agency, nor can it ever take place without me. I become through my relationship to the *Thou;* as I become *I,* I say *Thou.*" (Buber, M. *I and Thou.* New York: Scribner, 1958, 11.)
10. Durant, W. *The Story of Philosophy.* New York: *Washington Square Press,* 1961.
11. Kabbalistic tradition states that "God willed to see God" and so "God willed the first separation so that God might behold God." (Halevi, Z.S. *A Kabbalistic Universe.* York Beach, ME: Samuel Weiser, 1977, 7.)
12. "I AM that I AM" is the name of God given to Moses by God on Mount Sinai.(*Holy Bible.* King James version. Exodus 3:14)

Chapter 2

1. *Holy Bible.* Genesis 1:2
2. See Chapter 1: End Note 11.
3. Campbell, J. *The Mythic Image.* Princeton University Press, Princeton: Princeton University Press, 1974, 77.
4. Ibid.
5. Bierlein, J.F. *Parallel Myths.* New York: Ballantine, 1994.
6. *Holy Bible.* Genesis 1:3–4.
7. Eric Neumann informs us that "The Light" is the symbol of consciousness and "only in the light of consciousness can man know. And this act of cognition, of conscious discrimination, sunders the world into opposites, for experience of the world is only possible through opposites." (Neumann, E. *The Origins and History of Consciousness,* 104.)
8. Ibid., 104.
9. Jung, C. G. "The Meaning of Psychology for Modern Man."

Civilization in Transition: The Collected Works of C. G. Jung (Trans. R.F.C. Hull). Princeton: Princeton University Press, 1970.

10. Nadeau, R. & Kafatos, M. *The Non-Local Universe.* New York, Oxford University Press, 1999; Walker, E.H. *The Physics of Consciousness.*, Cambridge, MA: Perseus, 2000; Goswami, A. *The Self-Aware Universe.* New York: J. P. Tarcher /Putnam Books, 1993.

11. De Quincy, C. *Radical Nature.* Montpelier, VT: Invisible Cities Press, 2002.

12. Richard Tarnas addresses this in his overview of Thomas Aquinas's influence on Christian theology and its affect on Western culture in his book *The Passion of the Western Mind.* Aquinas believed "God willed each creature to move according to his own nature, with man himself given the greatest degree of autonomy by virtue of his rational intelligence. Man's freedom was not threatened either by natural laws or by his relationship to God, but rather was built into the fabric of the divinely created order." (Tarnas, R. *The Passion of the Western Mind.* New York: Ballantine Books, 1991, 180–181.)

13. The Original Sin of The Fall was celebrated as "O felix culpa!" ("Oh blessed sin!") in the Catholic Easter liturgy. As Tarnas informs us, "The Fall—man's primal error bringing the dark knowledge of good and evil, the moral perils of freedom, the experience of alienation and death—was here viewed not so much as an unmitigatedly heinous and tragic disaster, but as an early and, in retrospect, integral part of mann's existential development…" He adds further, "… [i]t was just through a painfully acute consciousness of this sin that man could now experience the infinite joy of God's forgiveness and embrace of his lost soul." (Tarnas, R. *The Passion of the Western Mind,* 126)

14. "Condemned" is the culturally conditioned adjective of choice. However, this word, like guilt and original sin, leads one to believe the fall from paradise was a punishment for a wrong action. In the context of creation, this separation was necessary for the development of self-awareness.

15. Neumann, E. The *Origins and History of Consciousness,* 117.

16. The term "maximal contrast" is adopted from mathematician G. Spencer-Brown from his book *Laws of Form.* In his book he discusses maximal contrast as a creative principle. To quote him, "… [A] universe comes into being when a space is severed or taken

apart. The skin of a living organism cuts off an outside from an inside. So does the circumference of a circle in a plane. By tracing the way we represent such a severance, we can begin to reconstruct, with an accuracy and coverage that appear almost uncanny, the basic forms underlying linguistic, mathematical, physical, and biological science, and can begin to see how the familiar laws of our own experience follow inexorably from the original act of severance." (Spencer-Brown, G. "Introduction: A Note on the Mathematical Approach." *Laws of Form.* New York: E.P. Dutton, 1979, xxix–xxx.)

17. Spencer-Brown, G. *Laws of Form,* 1979; Tenen, S. "The God of Abraham, A Mathematician's View: Is There Mathematical Argument for the Existence of God?" *The Noetic Journal,* 1999;2(2).

18. Tenen, S. "The God of Abraham...," *The Noetic Journal,* 1999; 2(2).

19. Neumann clarifies this when he states, "The opposition between light and darkness has informed the spiritual world of all peoples and molded it into shape. The sacred world order and the sacred space—precinct or sanctuary—were 'oriented' by this opposition. Not only man's theology, religion, and ritual, but the legal and economic orders that later grew out of them, the formation of the state and the whole pattern of secular life, down to the notion of property and its symbolism, are derived from this act of discrimination and the setting of boundaries made possible by the coming of light." (Neumann, E. *The Origins and History of Consciousness,* 107.)

20. String theory is elegantly and thoroughly discussed in physicist Brian Greene's book *The Elegant Universe.* These tiny strings of matter are thought to be the "absolute smallest constituents of anything and everything." They form vibrating loops of various sizes and, therefore, various frequencies. The different frequencies determine the nature of the particles of matter. The length of a typical string loop is about a hundred billion billion times smaller than an atomic nucleus. (Greene, B. *The Elegant Universe.* New York: Norton & Company, 1999, 141.)

21. Neumann, E. *The Origins and History of Consciousness,* 1954.

22. G. Spencer Brown informs us, "We can not escape the fact that the

world we know is constructed in order (and thus in such a way as to be able) to see itself but in order to do so, evidently it must first cut itself up into at least one state which sees, and at least one other state which is seen." (Brown, G. S. *Laws of Form*, 1979.)

23. "If the Holy One had not created a spirit of good that emanates from the active light, and spirit of evil that emanates from the passive light or darkness, man would have been a neutral ignorant kind of being unable to distinguish and contrast things essential to mental growth and spiritual development and progress." (*Zohar.* Trans. N. De Manhar. San Diego: Wizards Books, 1978, 119.)

24. In his book *The Conscious Mind,* Chalmers states, "Where there is awareness, there is consciousness and where there is consciousness there is awareness." (Chalmers, D. *The Conscious Mind.* New York: Oxford University Press, 1996, 222.)

25. "Without the immanent world of manifestation, there would be no soul, no self that experiences itself as separate from the object it perceives." (Goswami, A. *The Self-Aware Universe*, 188.)

26. Personal conversation with Christian de Quincy, Ph.D. in Seattle, October, 26, 2002. As professor of cosmology and consciousness at JFK University, he teaches that consciousness *in*forms and *en*forms matter. His book *Radical Nature* presents a new and "radical" theory of consciousness supporting the idea that consciousness is the *materia prima* of the universe. (De Quincy, C. *Radical Nature.* Montpelier, VT: Invisible Cities Press, 2002.

27. Neumann addresses this when he states, "There falls to man and to man alone, the essential mark of 'relatedness' because he as an individual, enters into relations with an object, be it another person, a thing, the world, his own soul, or God. He then becomes part of a higher and qualitatively different unity, which is no longer the pre-egoid unity of uroboboric containment, but an alliance in which the ego, or rather the self, the totality of the individual, is preserved intact. But this new unity is likewise based on the 'opposition' that came into the world with the separation of the World Parents and the dawning of ego consciousness." (Neumann, E. *The Origins and History of Consciousness,* 116.)

28. Buber, M. *I and Thou,* 109.

29. This is a Sanskrit expression from the Hindu *Chândogya Upanishad,* 8th century B.C. Campbell, J. Ed. E. C. Kennedy.

Thou Art That: Transforming Religious Metaphor. Novato, CA: New World Library, 2001, 26.

30. Buber, M. *I and Thou,* 25.
31. Ibid., 11.
32. Baucum, D. *Psychology.* Hauppauge, NY: Barons Ed. Series, Inc., 1999, 91–93.
33. *Zohar.* Trans. N. De Manhar. San Diego: Wizards Books, 1978.
34. Schneider, M. *A Beginner's Guide to Constructing the Universe: The Mathematical Archetypes of Nature, Art, and Science.* New York: Harper Perennial, 1995.
35. Michel, J. *City of Revelation.* London: Sphere Books, 1972, 86.
36. "From the earliest of times, it has been respected as a symbol of the sacred marriage, with the spiritual world of essences as the circle on the right penetrating the world of material phenomena on the left." (Ibid., 87.)
37. See Chapter 2: End Note 10. "Our real and local world is immersed in and interpenetrated by a more basic reality that is invisible and nonlocal." This nonlocal world is the domain of the quantum wave function.(Friedman, N. *The Hidden Domain.* Eugene, OR: The Woodbridge Group, 1997, 92.)
38. Goswami, A. *The Self-Aware Universe,* 140; Wolinsky, S. *Quantum Consciousness.* Las Vegas: Bramble Books, 1993; Zohar, D. *The Quantum Self.* New York: Quill/William Morrow, 1990.
39. Schneider, M. *A Beginner's Guide to Constructing the Universe,* 32.
40. Campbell, J. *The Hero With A Thousand Faces.* Princeton, NJ: Princeton Univ. Press, 1973, 280.
41. Rumi, J. "When a Man and a Woman Become One." *Love Is a Stranger. Selected Lyric Poetry of Jelaluddin Rumi.* Trans. K. Helminski. Putney, VT: Threshold Books, 1993, 54-55.
42. Gibran, K. "Marriage." *The Prophet.* New York: Knopf, Inc., 1951, 15–16.
43. "In the eyes of him who takes his stand in love, and gazes out of it, men are cut free from their entanglement in bustling activity. Good people and evil, wise and foolish, beautiful and ugly, become successively real to him; that is, set free they step forth in their singleness and confront him as *Thou.*" (Buber, M. *I And Thou,* 15.)
44. Writings of St. Symeon the Younger, 949–1022 A.D.

45. "Being 'embraces' itself and nonbeing. Being has nonbeing 'within' itself as that which is eternally present and eternally overcome in the process of the divine life." (Tillich, P. *The Courage To Be,* 34)

Chapter 3

1. Neumann, E. *The Origins and History of Consciousness,* 109.
2. Eisler, R. *The Chalice And The Blade.* San Francisco: Harper Collins, 1987; Campbell, J. *The Mythic Image,* 1974; Campbell, J. "Mythos: From Goddess to God." Videotape. Joseph Campbell Foundation, 1996.
3. Campbell, J. "Mythos: From Goddess to God." Videotape. Joseph Campbell Foundation, 1996.
4. See Chapter 3: End Note 2. Bierlein, J.F. *Parallel Myths,* 1994.
5. Tarnas, R. *The Passion of the Western Mind,* 142
6. Eisler, R. *The Chalice And The Blade,* 1987; Neumann, *E. The Origins and History of Consciousness,* 1954; Campbell, J. *The Mythic Image,* 1974)
7. In that decision, Chief Justice, Roger B. Taney wrote, with reference to the historical relationship between European peoples and slaves of African descent: "They [Negros] had for more than a century before been regarded as beings of an inferior order, and altogether unfit to associate with the white race, either in social or political relations; and so far inferior, that they had no rights which the white man was bound to respect; and that the Negro might justly and lawfully be reduced to slavery for his benefit. He was bought and sold, and treated as an ordinary article of merchandise and traffic, whenever a profit could be made by it." ("The Dred Scott Decision," U.S. Supreme Court, 1857; Hopkins, V.C. *Dred Scott's Case.* New York: Fordham University Press, 1951.)
8. The contrasting characteristics of these two opposing models are delineated by Riane Eisler, an internationally acclaimed scholar, futurist, and activist, in her paradigm-shattering book *The Chalice and The Blade.* (Eisler, R. *The Chalice and The Blade,* 1987.)
9. Ibid.
10. Carey, K. *Return of the Bird Tribes.* San Francisco: Harper Books, 1991.
11. Tarnas, R. *The Passion of the Western Mind,* 165
12. Ibid., 241

13. Ibid., 192
14. Ibid.
15. Physicist Amit Goswami does an excellent job of defining, comparing and contrasting the philosophical view of material realism in scientific thought in his book *The Self-Aware Universe.* (Goswami, A. *The Self-Aware Universe,* 1993.)
16. To quote Rupert Sheldrake, Ph.D.(former scholar of Clare College, Cambridge, and Frank Knox Fellow at Harvard University), from his book *A New Science of Life:* "According to this modified philosophy of materialism, the universe is composed of matter and energy, which are either eternal or of unknown origin, organized into an enormous variety of inorganic and organic forms which all arose by chance, governed by laws which cannot themselves be explained. Conscious experience is either an aspect of or runs parallel to the motor fields acting on the brain. All human creativity, like evolutionary creativity, must ultimately be ascribed to chance." (Sheldrake, R. *A New Science of Life.* Rochester, VT: Park Street Press, 1995, 201.)
17. Pert, C. *Molecules of Emotion.* New York: Scribner's Sons, 1997.
18. "In this sense all knowledge rests on an aggressive act of incorporation. The psychic system, and to an even greater extent consciousness itself, is an organ for breaking up, digesting, and then rebuilding the objects of the world and the unconscious, in exactly the same way as our bodily digestive system decomposes matter physiochemically and uses it for the creation of new structures." (Neumann, E. *The Origins and History of Consciousness,* 318.)

Chapter 4

1. As physicist Fritjof Capra states: "Quantum theory forces us to see the universe not as a collection of physical objects, but rather as a complicated web of relations between the various parts of a unified whole. This, however, is the way in which mystics have experienced the world, and some of them have expressed their experiences in words which are almost identical with those used by atomic physicists." (Capra, F. *The Tao of Physics.* Boulder, CO: Shambhala, 1975, 138.)
2. Bohm, D. *Wholeness and the Implicate Order.* London: Routledge

& Kegan Paul (ARK edition), 1983, 7.

3. Talbot, M. *The Holographic Universe.* New York: Harper Perennial, 1992; Goswami, A. *The Self-Aware Universe,* 1993; Gleick, J. *Chaos: Making of A New Science.* New York: Penguin, 1987; Hall, N. *Exploring Chaos.* New York: Norton & Company, 1991; Sheldrake, R. *A New Science of Life,* 1995; Capra, F. *The Web of Life,* 1996; Margulis, L. & Sagan, D. *What Is Life?* New York: Simon & Schuster, 1995; Lovelock, J. *Gaia.* New York: Harmony Books, 1979; Penrose, R. *Shadows of the Mind.* Oxford, UK: Oxford University Press, 1994.

4. Capra, F. *The Web of Life,* 36.

5. Ibid., 37.

6. Briggs, J. & Peat, D. *Turbulent Mirror.* New York: Harper & Row, 1989, 127.

7. Prigogine, I. & Stengers, I. *Order Out of Chaos.* New York: Bantam, 1984; Gleick, J. *Chaos: Making of A New Science,* 1987; Hall, N. *Exploring Chaos,* 1991; Briggs, J. & Peat, D. *Turbulent Mirror,* 1989.

8. Ibid.

9. Campbell, J. *The Hero With A Thousand Faces,* 297.

10. Excerpted from Arthur Koestler's book, *Janus: A Summing Up,* as it appears in Barlow, C. (Ed.) *From Gaia to Selfish Genes.* Cambridge, MA: MIT Press, 1998, 91.

11. Ibid., 98.

12. Ibid., 96.

13. As physicist Fritjof Capra elaborates, "Living systems are integrated wholes whose properties can not be reduced to those of smaller parts. Their essential, or 'systemic,' properties are properties of the whole, which none of the parts have. They arise from the 'organizing relations' of the parts." (Capra, F. *The Web of Life.* New York: Anchor, 1996, 36.)

Chapter 5

1. Gleick, J. *Chaos.* New York: Penguin Books, 1987, 103.

2. In the original Hebrew text, the Hebraic pleural form of the word for god (*Elohim*) is used where the italicized *our* is used in the English King James text.

3. Halevi, Z.S. *A Kabbalistic Universe,* 1977.

4. Greene, B. *The Elegant Universe,* 1999.
5. Greene, B. *The Elegant Universe,* 1999; Gribbin, J. *The Search for Superstrings, Symmetry, and the Theory of Everything.* New York: Little, Brown & Company, 1998; Bierlein, J.F. *Parallel Myths,* 1994; Campbell, J. *The Mythic Image,* 1974.
6. *Zohar.* Trans. N. De Manhar. San Diego: Wizards Books, 1978; Kaplan, A. *Sefer Yetzirah in Theory and Practice.* York Beach, ME: Weiser, 1991.
7. Halevi, Z.S. *A Kabbalistic Universe,* 1977, 7–8.
8. *The Book of the Dead,* Chapter LXIV, Papyrus of Nebseni. Trans. E.A.W. Budge & K. Paul. London: Trench, Trubner & Co., 1898, 112–113. Excerpted from Campbell, J. *The Mythic Image.* 1974, 17.
9. Nadeau, R. & Kafatos, M. *The Non-Local Universe,* 1999.
10. To quote physicist and founder of the Walker Cancer Institute, Evan Harris Walker, "… [T]he limit of our ability to observe the universe determines the boundaries of reality. Physical reality and observability are tied together." (Walker, E.H. *The Physics of Consciousness,* 54.)
11. *Zohar.* Trans. N. De Manhar, 1978, 85.
12. "Hymns of Creation." *Hymns From The Rig-Veda.* Trans. J. Le Mee. New York: Knopf, 1975.
13. Lao Tsu. *Tao Te Ching.* Trans. G. F. Feng & J. English. New York: Vintage, 1972, 32.
14. *Zohar.* Trans. N. De Manhar, 1978.
15. Neumann, E. *The Origins and History of Consciousness,* 12.
16. Halevi, Z.S. *A Kabbalistic Universe,* 7.
17. Campbell, J. *The Mythic Image,* 1974; Neumann, E. *The Origins and History of Consciousness,* 1954.
18. "In the beginning God created the heaven and the earth." (*Holy Bible:* Genesis 1:1)
19. Halevi, Z.S. *A Kabbalistic Universe,* 7–8
20. "And the earth was without form, and void; and darkness was upon the face of the deep. And the spirit of God moved upon the face of the waters." (*Holy Bible.* Genesis 1:2)
21. Briggs, J. & Peat, D. *Turbulent Mirror,* 1989; Prigogine, I. *The End of Certainty.* New York: The Free Press, 1996.
22. Genz, H. *Nothingness: The Science of Empty Space.* Reading, MA: Perseus Books, 1999.

23. Genz, H. *Nothingness: The Science of Empty Space,* 1999; Nadeau, R. & Kafatos, M. *The Non-Local Universe,* 1999.
24. Genz, H. *Nothingness: The Science of Empty Space,* 32.
25. Ibid.
26. Gribbin, J. *The Search for Superstrings, Symmetry, and the Theory of Everything,* 55–56.
27. Briggs, J. & Peat, D. *The Turbulent Mirror,* 1989; Gleick, J. *Chaos,* 1987.
28. "Hymn of Creation." *Hymns From The Rig-Veda.* Trans. J. Le Mee. New York: Knopf, 1975.
29. Neumann, E. *The Origins and History of Consciousness,* 12; *Holy Bible:* Genesis 1:2.
30. It is taught, in the tradition of Kabbalah, that the "Three Hidden Splendors" of creative intelligence are hidden in "The Spirit of God that moved upon the face of the waters." Will is one of these creative principles. (Halevi, Z.S. *A Kabbalistic Universe,* 1977.)
31. Tenen, S. "The God of Abraham…," *The Noetic Journal;* 2(2):1999.
32. The Meru Foundation and the work of its founder, Stan Tenen, provide a thorough discussion of this subject and the Kabbalistic, geometric, and mathematical metaphors of Biblical Genesis and the Hebraic letter-code that support it. We highly advise further exploring their work at . (Tenen, S. "The Meru Thesis and Scholarly Perspective." Meru Foundation, Sharon, MA, 1999)
33. *Holy Bible.* Genesis 2:19.
34. Ibid., Genesis 1:4.
35. *Zohar,* 87.
36. *Brihadaranyaka Upanishad,* 1. 4. 1–5. Trans. Swami M. Madhavananda, 1934.
37. Greene, B. *The Elegant Universe,* 4.
38. *Zohar,* 85.
39. Ibid., 87.
40. Greene, B. *The Elegant Universe,* 1999, 14.
41. Ibid., 16.

Chapter 6

1. Halevi, Z. S. *A Kabbalistic Universe,* 8.
2. Lao Tsu. *Tao Te Ching,* 42.

3. Kaplan, A. *Zefer Yetzirah,* 5.
4. Notes from personal studies with Edna Lister and The Society of the Universal Living Christ, Cleveland, OH, 1971–1981.
5. Bohm, D. *Wholeness and The Implicate Order,* 1983.
6. Capra, F. *The Web of Life,* 1996.
7. Ibid., 161.
8. Ibid.
9. Ibid.
10. Maturana, H. & Varela, F. *Autopoiesis and Cognition: The Realization of the Living.* Boston: Reidel, 1980; Maturana, H. & Varela, F. *The Tree of Knowledge.* Boston: Shambala, 1987.
11. Ibid.
12. Ibid.
13. Chalmers, D. *The Conscious Mind,* 1996.
14. Ibid., 172.
15. Ibid.
16. Capra, F. *The Web of Life,* 162.
17. Maturana, H. & Varela, F. *Autopoiesis and Cognition,* 1980; Maturana, H. and Varela, F. *The Tree of Knowledge,* 1987; Capra, F. *The Web of Life,* 1966.

Chapter 7

1. Sheldrake, R. *A New Science of Life.* Rochester, VT: Park Street Press, 1995, 60.
2. Ibid.
3. Genz, H. *Nothingness: The Science of Empty Space.* Reading, MA: Perseus Books, 1999.
4. Ibid., 12–13.
5. The DNA molecule consists of two antiparallel polynucleotide chains twisted into a right-handed double helix.(Frank-Kamenetskii, M.D. *Unraveling DNA.* Reading, MA: Addison-Wesley, 1997.)
6. Schneider, M. *A Beginner's Guide to Constructing the Universe,* 1995.
7. Ibid., 8.
8. Ibid., 4.
9. Neumann, E. *The Origins and History of Consciousness,* 11.
10. According to chemist Peter Coveney: "Many scientists are now

using nonlinear dynamics to model a dizzying range of complicated phenomena, from fluid dynamics, through chemical and biochemical processes, to genetic variation, heart beats, population dynamics, evolutionary theory and even into economics." (Coveney, P. "Chaos, Entropy and the Arrow of Time." *Exploring Chaos.* Ed. N. Hall. 1991, 209.)

11. Tenen, S. "The God of Abaham…," *The Noetic Journal*;2(2):1999, 192–204; Gleick, J. *Chaos: Making a New Science,* 1987; Briggs, J. & Peat, D. *The Turbulent Mirror,* 1989.

12. As John Briggs and David Peat inform us, "They [fractals] embrace not only the realms of chaos and noise but a wide variety of natural forms which the geometry that has been studied for the last two and a half thousand years has been powerless to describe forms such as coastlines, trees, mountains, galaxies, clouds, polymers, rivers, weather patterns, brains, lungs, and blood supplies." (Briggs, J. & Peat, D. *The Turbulent Mirror,* 1989, 91.)

13. Ibid., 106.

14. Prigogine, I. & Stengers, I. *Order Out of Chaos,* 1984; Prigogine, I. *The End of Certainty,* 1996.

15. Maturana, H. & Varela:, F. *Autopoiesis and Cognition,* 1980; Maturana, H. and Varela, F. *The Tree of Knowledge,* 1987.

16. Capra, F. *The Web of Life,* 1996; Prigogine, I. & Stengers, I. *Order Out of Chaos,* 1984.

17. *Holy Bible.* Exodus 3:13–14.

18. Ibid., Psalms 8:1.

19. Lao Tsu. *Tao Te Ching.*

20. Campbell, J. *The Hero With A Thousand Faces,* 266.

21. *Holy Bible:* John 10:30.

22. Ibid. Genesis 3:11.

23. Ibid. Genesis. 3:7–8.

24. Ibid. Genesis. 3:16–24.

25. Ibid. Genesis 1:11–12.

26. Ibid. Genesis 3:22.

Chapter 8

1. Prigogine, I & Stengers, I. *Order Out of Chaos,* 1984.

2. "Simply stated, [the Gaia] hypothesis says that the surface of the Earth, which we've always considered to be the *environment* of life,

is really *part* of life. The blanket of air—the troposphere—should be considered a circulatory system, produced and sustained by life. When scientists tell us that life adapts to an essentially passive environment of chemistry, physics, and rocks, they perpetuate a severely distorted view. Life actually makes and forms and changes the environment to which it adapts. Then that 'environment' feeds back on the life that is changing and acting and growing in it. There are constant cyclic interactions." (Margulis, L. "Gaia: The Living Earth." Dialogue with Fritjof Capra. *The Elmwood Newsletter;* 5(2): 1989.)

Lovelock, J. *Gaia,* 1979; Margulis, L. & Sagan, D. *What Is Life?* New York: Simon & Schuster, 1995; Capra, F. *The Web of Life,* 1996.

3. Coveney, P. "Chaos, Entropy and the Arrow of Time." In *Exploring Chaos.* Ed. N. Hall, 204.

4. Prigogine, I. & Stengers, I. *Order Out of Chaos,* 1984; Prigogine, I. *The End of Certainty: Time, Chaos and the New Laws of Nature,* 1997.

5. Systems that behave in this manner have been termed "dissipative structures" by Nobel laureate chemist Ilya Prigogine. Dissipative structures are dynamic, open systems whose dissipated energy becomes a source of order. These structures maintain themselves in a dynamically stable state far from equilibrium. They evolve as the flow of energy and matter into them from the outside world increases causing instabilities and chaos. They transform themselves through the chaos and self-organize into new structures of increased complexity. (Prigogine, I. & Stengers, I. *Order Out of Chaos,* 1984.)

6. Ibid., 13.

7. Ibid., 14.

8. Capra, F. *The Web of Life,* 83.

9. An excellent example of spontaneous self-organization in a chemical system is the Belousov-Zhabotinsky reaction discussed in chapter four. Another example is the Benard instability. This is a phenomenon occurring in liquid or gas solutions in which previously disordered whorls of convection currents spontaneously transform into an ordered lattice of hexagonal currents called "Benard cells." Prigogine, I. & Stengers, I. *Order Out of Chaos,* 1984; Briggs, J. & Peat, D. *Turbulent Mirror,* 1989, 137.

10. In this situation, the argument of the material realist might go something like this: "The physical pattern of organization is what determines a system's identity and consciousness which, in turn, determines its 'prime directive.' All conscious phenomena and identity are a result of the physical organization of a living system and that organization is further the result of random environmental influences."

11. Prigogine, I & Stengers, I. *Order Out of Chaos,* 1984; Prigogine, I. *The End of Certainty,* 1997; Schwartz, J. *Sudden Origins.* New York: John Wiley and Sons, 1999; Holland, J. *Hidden Order: How Adaptation Builds Complexity.* Reading, MA: Perseus Books, 1995.

12. Campbell, J. *The Mythic Journey,* 198.

13. Holland, J. *Hidden Order: How Adaptation Builds Complexity,* 1995.

14. Schrodinger, E. *What Is Life?* New York: Cambridge University Press, 1992, 100.

15. Hall, N., Ed. *Exploring Chaos,* 1991; Prigogine, I & Stengers, I. *Order Out of Chaos,* 1984.

16. Kauffman, S. "Antichaos and Adaptation." *Sci Amer,_*1991; 265: 78–84.

17. Capra, F. *The Web of Life,* 221.

18. Schrodinger, E. *What Is Life?* 1992, 101.

19. "In far-from-equilibrium conditions a system begins to be able to perceive, to 'take into account,' in its way of functioning, differences in the external world." (Prigogine, I. & Stengers, I. *Order Out of Chaos,* 14.)

20. "The concept of health cannot be defined without relation to its opposite—disease. But this is not merely a matter of definition. In reality, health is not health without the essential possibility and existential reality of disease. In this sense, health is disease conquered, as eternally the positive is positive by conquering the negative. This is the deepest theological significance of medicine.." (Tillich, P. *The Meaning of Health,* 1981.)

21. Ibid.

22. "Disease is a symptom of the universal ambiguity of life. Life must risk itself in order to win itself, but in the risking it may lose itself. A life which does not risk disease—even in the highest forms of the life of the spirit—is a poor life, as is shown, for instance, by the hypochondriac or the conformist.t." (Tillich, P. *The Meaning of Health,* 1981.)

23. Campbell, J. *The Hero With A Thousand Faces*, 25.

Chapter 9

1. Campbell, J. *The Hero With A Thousand Faces*, 39.
2. *Holy Bible*. Corinthians 15:31.
3. Marcus Aurelius, Roman Emperor and Stoic philosopher, 121—180 A.D..
4. Shakespeare, W. "As You Like It." Act 2; Scene 7.
5. "Only birth can conquer death—the birth, not of the old thing again, but of something new. Within the soul, within the body social, there must be—if we are to experience long surviva—a continuous 'recurrence of birth' (*palingenesia*) to nullify the unremitting recurrences of death." (Campbell, J. *The Hero With A Thousand Faces*, 16.)
6. Buber, M. *I And Thou*, 11.
7. Ibid., 10.
8. Campbell, J. *The Hero With A Thousand Faces*, 17.
9. In the classic Chinese book of life entitled *The Secret of the Golden Flower*, it is written that "When you turn the light around to shine inward, [the mind] is not aroused by things; negative energy then stops, and the flower of light radiates a concentrated glow, which is pure positive energy." (*The Secret of the Golden Flower*. Trans. T. Cleary, 1991, 41.)
10. Campbell, J. *The Hero With A Thousand Faces*, 1949.
11. Tillich, P. *The Courage To Be*, 28.
12. *Holy Bible*. Matthew 11:39.
13. Tillich, P. *The Courage To Be*, 1952.
14. Briggs, J. & Peat, D. *Seven Life Lessons of Chaos*. New York: Harper Collins, 1999, 30.
15. Kabasa, S. "Stressful life effects, personality and health: An inquiry into hardiness." *J Pers Soc Psychol* 1979; 37: 1–11.
16. Ibid.; Holland, J. *Hidden Order: How Adaptation Builds Complexity*, 1995.
17. Kabasa, S. "Stressful life effects, personality and health : An inquiry into hardiness." *J Pers Soc Psychol*, 1979; 37: 1–11; Ader, R., Ed. *Psychoneuroimmunology*. New York: Academic Press, 1981; Solomon, G. "Psychoneuroimmunology: Interactions between central nervous system and immune system." *J Neurosci Res*, 1987; 18: 1–9; Tecoma, E. & Huey, L. "Psychic distress and the immune

response." *Life Sciences,* 1985: 36: 1799–1812; Dorian, B. & Garfinkle, P. "Stress, immunity and illness—a review." *Psychological Med,* 1987; 17: 393-407; Pert, C. *Molecules of Emotion,* 1997.

18. Dorian, B. & Garfinkle, P. "Stress, immunity and illness—a review." *Psychological Med,* 1987; 17: 393–407.

19. Tillich eloquently contrasts these two choices as being expressions of either the "submissive self" or the "self-affirming self." "The submissive self is the opposite of the self-affirming self, even if it is submissive to a God. It wants to escape the pain of hurting and being hurt. The obedient self, on the contrary, is the self, which commands itself and 'risketh itself thereby'. In commanding itself it becomes its own judge and its own victim. It commands itself according to the law of life, the law of self-transcendence. The will, which commands itself, is the creative will. It makes a whole out of fragments and riddles of life. It does not look back, it stands beyond a bad conscience, it rejects the 'spirit of revenge' which is the innermost nature of self-accusation and of the conscience of guilt, it transcends reconciliation, for it is the will to power. In doing all this, the courageous self is united with life itself and its secret." (Tillich, P. *The Courage To Be,* 29–30.)

Chapter 10

1. Dethlefsen, T. & Dahlke, R. *The Healing Power of Illness,* 1991, 12–13.

2. Tillich reminds us of this paradox, revealing disease as an intrinsic part of life, when he states: "The ambiguity of life exists in every creative process. In every creative process of life, a destructive trend is implied; in every integrating process of life, a disintegrating trend; in every process toward the sublime, a profanizing trend." (Tillich, P. *The Meaning of Health.* North Atlantic Books, 1981.) This statement by Tillich is merely a modern expression of concepts posed by ancient Hindu philosophers, mystics, and theologians based on centuries of observation of the workings of nature and the universe.

3. Dethlefsen, T. & Dahlke, R. *The Healing Power of Illness,* 1991, 13.

4. Capra, F. *The Tao of Physics,* 1975, 145.

5. *Holy Bible.* John 12:25.

6. Lister, Edna. Notes from Edna Lister's lectures and personal studies through The Society of the Universal Living Christ, Cleveland,

Ohio, 1971–1981.

7.   *Holy Bible.* Revelation 20:14–15

8.   Dethlefsen, T. & Dahlke, R. *The Healing Power of Illness,* 1991.

9.   Locke, S., Ader, R., et al., Eds. *Foundations of Psychomeuroimmunology.* Hawthorne, NY: Aldine Pub. Co., 1985; Pert, C. *Molecules of Emotion,* 1997.

10. Pert, C. *Molecules of Emotion,* 1997.

11. Ibid.

12. Cloninger, C. R., Ed. *Personality and Psychopathology.* Washington, D.C.: American Psychiatric Press, Wash. D.C., 1999; Denollet, J. "Type D personality: A potential risk factor refined." *J Psychosom Res,* 2000; 49: 255–266; Friedman, H. "Long-term relations of personality and health: Dynamisms, mechanisms, tropisms." *J Personality,* 2000; 68: 1089–1107; Ferguson, E. "Hypochondriacal concerns and the five factor model of personality." *J Personality,* 2000; 68: 705–24; Booth-Kewley, S. & Vickers, R. "Associations between major domains of personality and health behavior." *J Personality,* 1994; 62: 281–298.

13. Ibid. Stanwyck, D. & Anson, C. "Is personality related to illness? Cluster profiles of aggregated data." *Advances,* 1986; 3: 4–15.

14. Solomon, G. "Psychoneuroimmunology: Interactions between central nervous system and immune system." *J Neurosci Res,* 1987;18: 1–9.

15. Raymond, C. "Distrust, rage may be 'toxic core' that puts 'type A' person at risk." *JAMA,* 1989: 261; 813.

16. Ibid.

17. The T-lymphocytes are processed through the thymus gland in early infancy, hence the T for thymus. The thymus gland controls the development of lymphoid tissue and immune response to foreign proteins in early infancy.

18. According to microbiologists Lynn Margulis and Dorion Sagan, "Competition in which the strong wins has been given a good deal more press than cooperation. But certain superficially weak organisms have survived in the long run by being part of collectives, while the so-called strong ones, never learning the trick of cooperation, have been dumped onto the scrap heap of evolutionary extinction. If symbiosis is as prevalent and as important in the history of life as it seems to be, we must rethink biology from the beginning." (Margulis, L. & Sagan, D. "Microcosmos," *From Gaia to Selfish*

Genes. Barlow, C., Ed. Cambridge, MA: MIT Press, 1998, 59.)

19. Ibid., 59.
20. Travis, J. "Outside influences: A cancer cell's physical environment controls its growth." *Science News*, 1997;152: 138–39.
21. Dethlefsen and Dahlke offer an excellent description of this cancerous process in their book, *The Healing Power of Illness:*
    "The more the ego divides itself off, the more it loses the sense of that whole of which it is still part. There arises in the ego the illusion that it can act alone. In reality there can be no real state of separation from the rest of the universe. It is something that exists only in our ego's imagination. To the extent that the 'I' boxes itself in, we lose our *religio*, our link with the original source of all being. At this point, then, the ego starts trying to satisfy its own needs, and dictates what path we are to follow. For the 'I', everything that serves to delimit and differentiate it further is all to the good, for every re-emphasis of its boundaries gives it a still clearer sense of itself. The only thing that the ego is afraid of is becoming 'all-one', for this would imply its own death. At great cost, therefore, and with much intelligence and plethora of good arguments, the ego defends its own existence, commandeering the most sacrosanct of theories and the most noble of intentions to that end. Its sole aim is to survive." (Dethlefsen, T. & Dahlke, R. *The Healing Power of Illness.* 1991, 246.)
22. Scientific American. *What You Need To Know About Cancer.* Freeman & Company, New York, 1997.
23. See Chapter 10: End Note 21.
24. *Holy Bible:* Matthew 12:33.

Chapter 11

1. *Holy Bible.* Hebrews 11:1.
2. Whyte, D. "Tilicho Lake." *Where Many Rivers Meet.* Many Rivers Press, Langley, WA, 1990.
3. Lister, Edna. Notes from Edna Lister's lectures and personal studies through The Society of the Universal Living Christ, Cleveland, Ohio, 1971–1981.
4. *Holy Bible.* John 12:32.
5. Campbell, J. *The Hero With A Thousand Faces,* 17.
6. Ibid., 40.
7. Ibid., 40.

Bibliography & Credits

Ader, R., Ed. *Psychoneuroimmunology.* New York: Academic Press, 1981.

Baucum, D. *Psychology.* Hauppauge, NY: Baron's Ed. Series, Inc., 1999.

Bierlein, J.F. *Parallel Myths.* New York: Ballantine, 1994.

Bohm, D. *Wholeness and The Implicate Order.* London: Routledge & Kegan, 1983.

Booth-Kewley, S. & Vickers, R. "Associations between major domains of personality and health behavior." *J Personality,* 1994; 62: 281–298.

Briggs, J. & Peat, D. *Seven Life Lessons of Chaos.* New York: Harper Collins, 1999.

Ibid. *Turbulent Mirror.* New York: Harper & Row, 1989.

Brihadaranyaka Upanishad, 1. 4. 1–5. Trans. Swami Mayavati Madhavananda, 1934.

Buber, M. *I and Thou.* New York: Scribner's Sons, 1958.

Campbell, J. *Mythos: From Goddess to God.* Videotape. Joseph Cambell Foundation, 1996.

Ibid. *The Hero With A Thousand Faces.* Princeton: Princeton University Press, 1973.

Ibid. *The Mythic Image.* Princeton: Princeton University Press, 1974.

Ibid. *Transformations of Myth Through Time.* New York: Harper & Row, 1990.

Capra, F. *The Web of Life.* New York: Anchor Books, 1996.

Ibid. *The Tao of Physics.* Boulder, CO: Shambhala, 1975.

Carey, K. *Return of the Bird Tribes.* San Francisco: Harper Collins, 1991.

Chalmers, D. *The Conscious Mind.* New York: Oxford University Press, 1996.

Chopra, D. *Quantum Healing*. New York: Bantam Books, 1989.

Cleary, T., Trans. *The Secret of the Golden Flower*. San Francisco: Harper Collins, 1991.

Cloninger, C.R., Ed. *Personality and Psychopathology*. Washington, D.C.: American Psychiatric Press, 1999.

Coveney, P: "Chaos, entropy and the arrow of time." *Exploring Chaos*. Ed. N. Hall. New York: Norton & Company, 1991.

Denollet, J. "Type D personality: A potential risk factor refined." *J Psychosom Res*, 2000; 49: 255–266.

Dethlefsen, T. & Dahlke, R. *The Healing Power of Illness*. Rockport, MA: Element Books, 1991.

de Quincy, C. *Radical Nature*. Montpelier, VT: Invisible Cities Press, 2002.

Dorian, B. & Garfinkle, P. "Stress, immunity and illness—a review." *Psychological Med*, 1987; 17: 393–407.

Dossey, L. *Space, Time & Medicine*. Boston: New Science Library/Shambhala, 1982.

Durant, W. *The Story of Philosophy*. New York: Washington Square Press, 1961.

Eisler, R. *The Chalice And The Blade*. San Francisco: Harper Collins, 1987.

Ferguson, E. "Hypochondriacal concerns and the five factor model of personality." *J Personality*, 2000; 68: 705–724.

Frank-Kamenetskii, M.D. *Unraveling DNA*. Reading, MA: Addison-Wesley, 1997.

Friedman, H. "Long-term relations of personality and health: Dynamisms, mechanisms, tropisms." *J Personality*, 2000; 68: 1089–1107.

Friedman, N. *The Hidden Domain*. Eugene, OR: The Woodbridge Group, 1997.

Genz, H. *Nothingness: The Science of Empty Space*. Reading, MA: Perseus Books, 1999.

Gibran, K. *The Prophet*. New York: Alfred A. Knopf, Inc., 1951.

Gleick, J. *Chaos: Making of A New Science*. New York: Penguin, 1987.

Goswami, A. *The Self-Aware Universe*. New York: J. P. Tarcher/Putnam Books, 1993.

Gray, W.G. *Quabalistic Concepts*. York Beach, ME: Samuel Weiser, 1977.

Greene, B. *The Elegant Universe*. New York: Norton & Company, 1999.

Gribbin, J. *The Search for Superstrings, Symmetry, and The Theory of Everything.* New York: Little, Brown & Company, 1998.

Halevi, Z.S. *Adam and the Kabbalistic Tree.* New York: Samuel Weiser, 1974.

Ibid. *A Kabbalistic Universe.* York Beach, ME: Samuel Weiser, 1977.

Ibid. *The Way of Kabbalah.* New York: Samuel Weiser, 1976.

Hall, N., Ed. *Exploring Chaos.* New York: Norton & Company, 1991.

Hopkins, V.C. *Dred Scott's Case.* New York: Fordham University Press, 1951.

Hawking, S.W. *A Brief History of Time.* New York: Bantam Books, 1988.

Holy Bible, King James Version.

Holland, J. *Hidden Order: How Adaptation Builds Complexity.* Reading, MA: Perseus Books, 1995.

Holme, B., Ed. *Bulfinch's Mythology.* New York: Viking Press, 1979.

Hymns From The Rig-Veda. Trans. J. Le Mee. New York: Knopf, 1975.

I Ching (The Book of Change). Trans. J. Blofeld. New York: Dutton & Company, 1965.

Jung, C.G. "The Meaning of Psychology for Modern Man." *Civilization in Transition, The Collected Works of C. G. Jung.* Trans. R.F.C. Hull. Princeton, N.J. Princeton University Press, 1970.

Kabasa, S. "Stressful life effects, personality and health: An inquiry into hardiness." *J Pers Soc Psychol*, 1979; 37: 1–11.

Kaplan, A. *Sefer Yetzirah (The Book of Creation).* New York: Samuel Weiser, 1990.

Kaplan, A. *The Handbook of Jewish Thought.* New York: Maznaim Pub., 1979.

Kauffman, S. "Antichaos and Adaptation." *Sci Amer,* Aug. 1991; 265: 78–84.

Knight, G. *A Practical Guide To Quabalistic Symbolism.* New York: Samuel Weiser, 1978.

Koestler, A. *Janus: A Summing Up.* Excerpt as it appears in *From Gaia to Selfish Genes.* Ed. C. Barlow. Cambridge, MA: MIT Press, 1998.

Lao Tsu. *Tao Te Ching.* Trans. G. F. Feng & J. English. New York: Vintage, 1972.

Lister, Edna. Notes from personal studies through The Society of the Universal Living Christ, Cleveland, OH, 1971–1981.

Lovelock, J. *Gaia.* New York: Harmony Books, 1979.

Margulis, L. & Sagan, D. *Microcosmos.* Excerpt as it appears in *From Gaia to Selfish Genes.* Ed. C. Barlow. Cambridge, MA: MIT Press, 1998.

Ibid. *What Is Life?* New York: Simon & Schuster, 1995.

Maturana, H. & Varela, F. *Autopoiesis and Cognition: The Realization of the Living.* Boston: Reidel, 1980.

Ibid. *The Tree of Knowledge.* Boston: Shambala, 1987.

Michel, J. *City of Revelation.* London: Garnstone Press, 1972.

Milton, R. *Shattering the Myths of Darwinism.* Rochester: Park Street Press, 1997.

Nadeau, R. & Kafatos, M. *The Non-Local Universe.* New York: Oxford University Press, 1999.

Neumann, E. *The Origins and History of Consciousness.* Princeton: Princeton University Press, 1954.

Penrose, R. *Shadows of The Mind.* Oxford, England: Oxford University Press, 1994.

Ibid. *The Large, The Small And The Human Mind.* Oxford University Press, Oxford, England, 1997.

Pert, C. *Molecules of Emotion.* New York: Scribner's Sons, 1997.

Prigogine, I. *The End of Certainty.* New York: The Free Press, 1996.

Prigogine, I. & Stengers, I. *Order Out of Chaos.* New York: Bantam, 1984.

Raymond, C. "Distrust, rage may be "toxic core" that puts "type A" person at risk." *JAMA*, 1989; 261: 813.

Robinson, J. M., Ed. *The Nag Hammadi Library.* San Francisco: Harper Collins, 1990.

Rumi, J. *Love Is a Stranger: Selected Lyric Poetry of Jelaluddin Rumi.* Trans. Kabir Helminski. Putney, VT: Threshold Books, 1993.

Schneider, M. *A Beginner's Guide to Constructing the Universe. The Mathematical Archetypes of Nature, Art, and Science.* New York: Harper Perennial, 1995.

Schrodinger, E. *What Is Life?* New York: Cambridge University Press, 1992.

Schwartz, J.H. *Sudden Origins: Fossils, Genes, and The Emergence of Species.* New York: Wiley & Sons, 1999.

Scientific American. *What You Need To Know About Cancer.* New York: Freeman & Company, 1997.

Sheldrake, R. *A New Science of Life.* Rochester, VT: Park Street Press, 1995.

Solomon, G. "Psychoneuroimmunology: Interactions between central nervous system and immune system." *J Neurosci Res,* 1987; 18: 1–9.

Spencer-Brown, G. *Laws of Form.* New York: E.P. Dutton, 1979.

Stanwyck, D. & Anson, C. "Is Personality Related to Illness? Cluster profiles of aggregated data." *Advances,* 1986; 3: 4–15.

Talbot, M. *The Holographic Universe.* New York: Harper Perennial, 1992.

Tarnas, R. *The Passion of the Western Mind.* New York: Ballantine Books, 1991.

Tecoma, E. & Huey, L. "Psychic distress and the immune response." *Life Sciences,* 1985: 36: 1799–1812.

Tenen, S. "The God of Abraham, A Mathematician's View: Is There Mathematical Argument for the Existence of God?" *The Noetic Journal,* 1999; 2(2).

Ibid. "The Meru Thesis and Scholarly Perspective." Meru Foundation, Sharon, MA, 1999 / www.meru.org

The Book of the Dead, Chapter LXIV, Papyrus of Nebseni. Trans. E.A.W. Budge. London: Kegan Paul, Trench, Trubner & Co., 1898.

Tillich, P. *The Courage To Be.* New Haven, CT: Yale Univ. Press, 1952.

Idib. *The Meaning of Health.* Berkeley: North Atlantic Books, 1981.

Travis, J. "Outside influences: A cancer cell's physical environment controls its growth." *Science News,* 152: 138–139, 1997.

Waite, A. E. *The Holy Kabbalah.* Secaucus, NJ: University Books, 1975.

Walker, E. H. *The Physics of Consciousness.* Cambridge, MA: Perseus, 2000.

Whyte, D. "Tilicho Lake." *Where Many Rivers Meet.* Langley, WA: Many Rivers Press, 1990.

Wolf, F.A. *The Spiritual Universe.* Portsmouth, NH: Moment Point Press, 1999.

Wolinsky, S. *Quantum Consciousness.* Las Vegas: Bramble Books, 1993.

Zohar, D. *The Quantum Self: Human Nature and Consciousness Defined By The New Physics.* New York: Quill/William Morrow, 1990.

Zohar. Trans. N. De Manhar. San Diego: Wizards Books, 1978.

Credits

Index

A

Absolute All 3, 77, 81, 85, 89
actualization 195, 208. *See also* self-actualization
    hierarchies 47, 50
Adam and Eve 24, 90, 135
adaptation 75, 145, 165, 171, 192, 194, 207
affirmation 9, 14, 139, 167, 176, 182, 206
Age of Reason 55, 56
aleph 85, 120
anxiety 2, 9, 10, 14, 15, 49, 50, 157, 168, 169, 182
Aquinas 23
archetype 3, 13, 14, 36, 47, 51, 52, 90, 113–138
Aristotle 84, 114
Ark of the Covenant 85, 87
asymmetry 26, 28, 75, 80, 109, 119
atoms 30, 115
autocatalyze 82, 130, 148
autoimmune 182, 190, 191, 193
autopoiesis 104, 105–111, 141
awareness 31, 148, 210
    development of 131
    environmental / ecological 63
    of continuous creation 181
    of inside (self) and outside (nonself) 31
    of opposites and separate things 31
    of self 33. *(see also* self-awareness*)*
    of separateness 31, 33
    of the "mind-body" connection 64
    of the "other" 31
    state of 45

B

Belousov-Zhabotinsky 82
beth 120
Bible/Biblical 24, 90, 121, 134
Big Bang 77, 93, 117
birth 7, 19, 20, 29, 58, 63, 77, 79, 90, 134, 141, 155, 164–167, 170, 179
Bissell, Mina 197
blood of the lamb 101
Bohm, David 64, 100
Brahma 21
Brahman 21
Briggs, John 66, 126, 170
Buber, Martin 34 35, 42, 167

C

Campbell, Joseph 39, 46, 134, 163, 164, 166, 168, 211
cancer 180, 182, 189, 193, 195–201

Capra, Fritjof 65, 103, 104, 107, 148, 152, 179
catharsis 167
Catholic Church 24, 52, 54
Chalmers, David 31, 106, 107
chaos 10, 14, 16, 20, 25, 26, 28, 59, 60, 63, 64, 66, 71, 77, 79, 80, 81, 86, 109, 115, 116, 123, 126, 128, 141–162, 170, 171, 174, 175, 176, 177, 180, 181, 183, 184, 185, 192, 194, 199, 201, 206, 207
    chaos theory 64, 122
    edge of 141–162, 166, 173
    transformation through 70, 150
choice 21, 22, 23, 24, 90, 123, 173, 193, 200, 210, 212. *See also* choosing
    free 22, 23, 24, 74, 102, 123, 126, 135
choosing 22, 23, 24, 202
Christianity 9
circle 29, 35, 36, 37, 79, 84, 86, 91, 92, 98, 101, 109, 118, 119, 120, 121, 122, 123
co-creator 74
cognition 106, 131
compassion 51, 52, 53, 169, 210, 211
complexity 82, 114, 115, 123, 152, 154
    (increasing) 10, 68, 69, 75, 91, 114, 119, 130, 143, 145, 146, 147, 148, 150, 151, 155, 161, 164, 176, 180, 184
conception 85–87
consciousness XIX, XX, 1, 2, 15, 22, 23, 28, 31, 48, 51, 52 58, 59, 65, 78, 90, 96, 107, 129, 133, 143, 147, 148, 150, 153, 161, 164, 175, 181, 182, 187, 193, 195, 198, 205. *See also* self-consciousness
    and the physical body 187
    as a process 32, 33
    as embodiment of life 7, 8, 161
    autopoiesis 106, 107, 110, 111
    autopoiesis as a function of 106
    cognition, ties to 106
    corporate-industrial 200
    cultural 186
    definition of 31, 32
    disordered 202
    effects of 116
    ego-consciousness (egoic-consciousness) 3, 9, 20, 21, 47, 49, 60, 68, 90, 91, 133, 134, 135, 137
    evolutionary journey of 17, 23, 24, 59, 70
    familial 186, 201
    field of 100
    formation of 31
    global 186